A SIMPLIFIED APPROACH

TO SHAKESPEARE'S
Hamlet

By George R. Price

MICHIGAN STATE UNIVERSITY

BARRON'S EDUCATIONAL SERIES, INC.

GREAT NECK, NEW YORK

© 1964 by Barron's Educational Series, Inc.
343 GREAT NECK ROAD
GREAT NECK, NEW YORK

All rights are strictly reserved. Todos Derechos Reservados. No part of this book may be used or reproduced in any manner whatsoever without written permission except in the case of brief quotations embodied in critical articles and reviews.

Library of Congress Catalog Card No. 63–16880

PRINTED IN THE UNITED STATES OF AMERICA

CONTENTS

TO THE STUDENT	v
The Persons of the Play	1
A Commentary on the Action	7
Act I 7	
Act II 27	
Act III 37	
Act IV 48	
Act V 54	
A Summary of the Action	63
Act I 63	
Act II 65	
Act III 67	
Act IV 70	
Act V 72	
A Sampling of *Hamlet* Criticism	75
APPENDIX	81
A. The Melancholy Humor 81	
B. The Quartos and First Folio 83	
C. For Further Reading 85	
NOTES	86

To the Student

Shakespeare's *Hamlet,* the most famous of all tragedies, is also the most subject to varied interpretations. The discussion has added to the world's stock of innocent pleasure, though the mere volume of printed words now begins to have its evil aspects. (Ten books and articles on *Hamlet* per year for the last seventy-five years is certainly a conservative estimate.) Much of the criticism is founded on too little knowledge, and is negligible.

Since no scholar ever claims to have read all this volume of scholarly investigation and criticism, but only to have selected from it, the "Commentary" on *Hamlet* which you find in this book necessarily represents opinion based upon study within limits, notably the limits of about fifteen years of teaching Shakespeare and many more years of study of Elizabethan drama in general. You may expect that your instructor will differ at certain points from the interpretation given herein. In these cases your obligation by examination-time is to have studied the scenes in question very carefully and, if possible, to have read some interpretation of them. A few bibliographical suggestions are given in the "Appendix" to this book.

In using the "Commentary" in this book you will do well to re-read the lines in the play that are cited in the discussion. You may sometimes find the lines gaining a meaning you had not previously suspected. At any rate they are usually crucial lines, and reading them again will familiarize you with certain important aspects of the play that you need to know. The text of *Hamlet* that is referred to here is that found in *The Complete Plays and Poems of William Shakespeare,* edited by Neilson and Hill, 1942. If you are using another anthology of Shakespeare or edition of *Hamlet,* you may find that line numbers (especially of prose passages) do not correspond with the ones given here. But they probably will not be very different. You may be able to work out a simple ratio to make the cited numbers apply to your text.

In preparing the "Commentary" on *Hamlet* I have tried to approach the play as an acted play, specifically one acted at the

Globe Theater about 1601. This is not the only legitimate critical approach, but it is sound because it assumes that Shakespeare, knowing his play must be interpreted by an audience in a theater, would make the essential elements of his drama clear to those witnesses, and not leave the secret of his play to be dug out by readers at their desks. But please note that your study-problem is not much simplified by this approach. Besides needing a general conception of the structure of the Elizabethan stage, you are also to some extent involved with matters of costume, technique of acting, dramatic conventions, symbolism—not to speak of revenge tragedy and the *Ur-Hamlet,* the lost Hamlet play which preceded Shakespeare's, and which had familiarized Englishmen with the story. It is to be expected that your instructor will discuss the literary tradition from which *Hamlet* is derived.

Finally, out of the many topics of interpretation, even of controversy, which this tragedy furnishes, it may be helpful to distinguish eleven that seem to demand attention:

MAJOR CRITICAL DIFFICULTIES

1. Hamlet's sanity (the relations of melancholy, "antic disposition," and hysteria; see especially the "Commentary" on I.5 and the "Appendix").

2. The origin and authority of the Ghost.

3. Hamlet's delay or punctuality in revenging.

4. The influence of Senecan and revenge tragedy tradition upon the play.

5. Hamlet's success or failure, including his guilt or innocence.

MINOR CRITICAL PROBLEMS

1. The meaning of the Second Soliloquy (*To be or not to be*).
2. The meaning of the Apostrophe on Man.
3. The staging of the Mouse-Trap Scene.
4. The significance of the Prayer Scene.
5. The significance of the Closet Scene.
6. The staging of the duel.

If your text does not furnish you with a description of the Elizabethan stage, you will find a concise treatment of the matter in my *Reading Shakespeare's Plays,* which also has some suggestions on technique for study of the plays.

G. R. P.

The Persons of the Play

It is interesting, though not at all vital for appreciation of the play, that the large cast of characters certainly required the Lord Chamberlain's Men, the company to which Shakespeare belonged, to use the device of "doubling," by which actors played two or even more parts. (The exits and re-entries of these characters would have to be widely enough separated to allow for change of costumes.) For instance, Francisco, Reynaldo, and the Priest could have been played by one actor, Marcellus and Fortinbras by another.

As we glance at the list, we may be struck by the mingling of Germanic, Latin, and Italian names. The literary sources of *Hamlet* account for the incongruity; the ancient Norse saga furnished the Germanic names, but traditions of revenge tragedy account for the presence of Italian and Latin forms. As commonly in Shakespeare, there are ironic overtones in some of the names which make a comment on the persons: Rosencrantz ("crown of roses"), Guildenstern ("gold star"), Laertes (the aged, forlorn father of wandering Odysseus), Fortinbras ("strong arm"?), Gertrude (virgin and martyr). But others appear to be without special significance, and we are unable to say with certainty why Shakespeare chose them: Claudius (the Emperor who established Roman rule in Britain), Polonius ("the Pole").

CLAUDIUS, king of Denmark when the play begins, is brother of the late King Hamlet, whom Claudius secretly poisoned. Claudius is a *sensual, power-loving, sagacious, hypocritical, determined, treacherous* man, with *enough courage* to commit murder, but not enough to defy public opinion or to fight hard when cornered. Yet he has elements of virtue in him: habits of *decisive action*, of *self-control*, of *handling people politicly* or tactfully, of being *honest with himself*. He truly *loves* Queen Gertrude, whom he seduced when she was King Hamlet's wife. Claudius's keen *intelligence* makes him a dangerous foe.

GERTRUDE, both sister-in-law and wife of Claudius, is apparently as *sensual* as he, but *less intelligent* and determined. Unaware that her lover has slain her husband, King Hamlet, she can enjoy her second marriage with only slight twinges of remorse about her previous adultery and her hasty remarriage. She has stifled her conscience to the point that it is almost (but not quite) dead, and she can now enjoy life very well. She *loves* Claudius and her son Hamlet and is unhappy that they are not friends; she thinks the Prince's marriage to Ophelia may make him content. Gertrude combines sensuality with *amiable good will* to others and shows herself possessed of *physical courage*.

In the usual pattern of revenge tragedy Gertrude does not well fit a conventional part. She is too kind to be a villainess, too guilty to be the pitiful victim of the usurper, too maternal to her son to be a suitable object of his invective satires. She is both victim and ally of the antagonist, Claudius.

POLONIUS, chief adviser to Claudius, is the nobleman by whose help Claudius has been able to possess himself of the throne that the Danish people expected Prince Hamlet to inherit (through election by the nobility). Polonius is a *vain, garrulous, domineering, overcurious* old man now falling into dotage and losing his awareness of other people's reaction to his devices; but he retains enough of his former *cunning* and his reputation for *loyalty* to the crown so that both the nobility of the kingdom and Claudius himself have relied on him. Polonius has always been essentially *mundane* in his scale of values, but he has also been *averse to cruelty* and outright force.

The character of HAMLET is the chief critical problem of the play, and many have called it an insoluble enigma. However, some traits may safely be ascribed to him: As we find him during the course of the play, Hamlet has a *lively sense of humor* and a gift for expressing it *wittily*. He is *brave* and, at least in moments of peril, acts coolly and decisively. Hamlet's *idealism* still survives despite the shock of his mother's indecent marriage and even the shocks given him by the Ghost's revelations; he highly admires Horatio's, Fortinbras's, and even Laertes's manly virtues. Hamlet has a habit of *constant reflection* (of which, in some degree, his sense of humor is the result). An attractive aspect of his reflectiveness is his *enthusiasm for the art of drama,* which, as he says, *holds the mirror up to [human] nature* and so corrects our notions of ourselves; a less admirable aspect of his reflectiveness is his *agonizing introspection*. Hamlet's masterful *power of expression* employs words in a style that is *colloquial, vivid,* and *pithy*. As a result of this expressiveness he is *loquacious* and even berates himself for

The Persons of the Play

talking so much and to such small effect. To all these qualities are to be added the effects of his disease of melancholy; they are discussed in the "Commentary" on I.5 and in Appendix A. The preceding list has been confined to the traits which endure in spite of the onset of melancholy.

What Hamlet was before his father's death is sketched for us by Ophelia in III.1.158-168: He was a *lover of elegance* in behavior and expression, and a young man who must have had the *intelligence* and *diligence* to study all the knowledge proper to a scholar, courtier, and soldier, whose vocations are combined in the ideal prince. If Ophelia overestimates Hamlet's accomplishments a little, still there is no need for us to reject the portrait entirely. We know, of course, that he was a university student, and his excellence of character is evidence for us by the unanimous liking and friendship he has received, a feeling that even Claudius appears to wish to offer him.

In terms of conventional Elizabethan revenge tragedy Hamlet of course has the function of revenging the murder of his father, the seduction of his mother, and his own loss of the Danish throne.[1] Claudius's crimes of adultery and murder, if known to the world, would rob Hamlet of almost all the honor due to a gentleman as long as Hamlet allowed the criminal to live. Although the world does not know these injuries, Hamlet feels them as if they were known. For justice, his revenge must be bitter and complete; but his duty also is to recover his lost kingdom safely. Hence, seen in the traditions of revenge tragedy, Hamlet's position is necessarily ambiguous: He is a man deeply injured and therefore deserving of sympathy; but he is also a hater of his enemy and pursuer of covert revenge regardless of civil and moral law, and therefore deserving of condemnation.

Please note that the preceding description of Hamlet's function is oversimplified; the Prince in this play is *not* merely a hero-villain of revenge tragedy. Hamlet is uniquely individualized. But the Elizabethan audience's acceptance of the pattern of revenge tragedy was something Shakespeare could not, or did not, choose to ignore. Although Hamlet is as far from being a stereotype as any character in world drama, his behavior (but not his character) reminds us at times of other revengers in such plays as *The Spanish Tragedy, The Malcontent,* and *The Revenger's Tragedy.*

OPHELIA, submissive daughter of Polonius, has been in love with Hamlet, and he with her, until King Hamlet's death and Hamlet's resulting melancholy. Ophelia is a *virtuous, loving* girl, qualities which probably attracted Hamlet to her at first. But she is *obedient* to Polonius with a *meekness* which finally disgusts Hamlet and alienates us. Yet her conversation shows that Shakespeare did not intend an effect of stupidity, which in fact would have repelled Hamlet long ago. It is better to see her as merely *far too compliant* to a senile father. Her fate is to be the wretched victim of Polonius's dominance and Hamlet's melancholia.

LAERTES, unlike Hamlet, slips very easily into the role of revenger; for Laertes is pretty much a familiar type of the young aristocrat, *eager to enjoy life, supersensitive about his reputation* for mastery of the rapier and for honor, *unrestrained* by any control of morality once his honor has been affronted. Shakespeare had plenty of opportunity to observe such gentlemen in life, not merely on the stage. But Laertes's fits of *strong passion* seem genuine. His sobs of grief for Ophelia lead us to believe that his shouts of fury against the killer of Polonius express real sorrow for his father, not just shame for the disgrace of his hasty burial.

In terms of plot, and apart from his being a foil to Hamlet in *impetuosity* and *ruthlessness,* Laertes is molded by Claudius into the useful *tool* which the usurper in a revenge play needs to have at hand for plotted murders.

HORATIO is the bosom friend needed by the hero of revenge tragedy. (That hero is necessarily isolated with but few friends or none at all, as he lays his plot in the hostile environment of the usurper's court. Note, however, that Hamlet never comes to the point of laying any more plot than the presenting of the play-within-the-play.) The hero must have a confidant, and Horatio serves for this. In fact, as revenger, Hamlet is unusually isolated. Therefore, despite his frequent soliloquies, we need Horatio's *normal responses* in order to measure the truth in Hamlet's view of things. This is why Horatio appears and disappears; he is serving his dramatic function at need, not behaving realistically like a devoted friend who will not be parted from the hero's side. As confidant Horatio must be *faithful, trustworthy, loving,* and *prudent;* and so he is. These good qualities point to another aspect of Horatio's function, to *contrast to Hamlet's character* and thereby to make it more clear, vivid, and interesting. As *foil,* or contrast, Horatio appears *stable in temperament, self-controlled,* disciplined in *Stoic* philosophy. He is *impassive* to the whims of Fortune, whether good or bad.

The Persons of the Play

Shakespeare also finds Horatio useful as first interviewer of the Ghost; by this means the Ghost is introduced personally into the play, and Hamlet's interview with him is prepared for. In these scenes we find Horatio displaying *intelligence,* a tendency toward *reflectiveness,* and a *sense of humor.* Like Hamlet he has been a university student.

THE GHOST of the elder Hamlet is not just mechanism of plot or a device for thrilling the audience with horror; he is also a character. As do a few spectres in Seneca's Roman tragedies, the apparitions in earlier Elizabethan revenge plays come back to prompt the hero by demanding revenge. King Hamlet's Ghost, then, is a conventional figure; but Shakespeare humanizes him by endowing him with such passions as *love* for Hamlet and Gertrude, *grief* for Gertrude's sins, and *sorrow* for his loss of the last sacraments at death. Through these emotions, as well as Horatio's and Hamlet's description of the living King, we perceive a *brave, loving, trusting* man.

FORTINBRAS, a character not found in earlier versions of the Hamlet story, but added by Shakespeare, serves at least two functions, to be a foil to Hamlet (as are Horatio and Laertes) and to be King of Denmark after Hamlet's death. For which purpose Shakespeare first conceived the new character it is probably useless to speculate; the two functions are about equally significant in the play. Naturally, the contrast to Hamlet, which the Prince himself emphasizes in IV.4, appears first, as early as I.1.80-104.[2] Fortinbras, we learn, is *decisive, brave* even to foolhardiness, and *determined,* these qualities being manifested in a military expedition originally conceived as a result of his *love of honor.* Eagerness to regain honor lost by his father causes Fortinbras to fail in his duty to his King (by omitting to get permission for the raid on Denmark) and induces him to lead his company of *landless resolutes* to attack Poland sheerly for glory, with no hope of great plunder or gain of land. So high-colored is this picture of a glory-seeker that it verges on satire; Fortinbras seems to belong to the same class as Harry Hotspur. But considering *Hamlet* in its totality, and especially the last Act, we had better think of Fortinbras, not as a satire, but simply as a statement of real values in life much heightened for contrast to Hamlet. Otherwise, we may be forced to understand the play as condemning both Hamlet and Fortinbras in a spirit of cynicism which few critics feel is really its intention.

ROSENCRANTZ AND GUILDENSTERN are twins in character, though not in blood; they are indistinguishable in their *faithlessness* to Hamlet and *servility* to Claudius. Though they never convincingly express friendship for Hamlet or speak sympathetically about him to each other, we can in part excuse their first prying attempt to discover the cause of Hamlet's melancholy; for of course melancholia can be cured more easily if the cause is known. Naturally, their *commonplace thinking* is no match for Hamlet's wit. We dislike their *cold-hearted attitude* toward their boyhood friend and despise their *treachery* in conducting him to England, where they must guess, if they think at all, that his fate is likely to be imprisonment or something worse. For them and Claudius, Hamlet is the melancholy malcontent, a dangerous enemy of the King.

In terms of the revenge play Rosencrantz and Guildenstern are specimens of the corrupt nobility who surround a usurper and perform the criminal acts he commands; but these two are more ridiculous than the poisoners and stabbers who callously obey Italian princes, in other Elizabethan plays of this kind.

OSRIC, the *foolish courtier,* becomes the tool of Claudius and Laertes unawares. In terms of plot he scarcely counts more than Reynaldo or the Grave-diggers; he is a servant of villains, but too *naïve* to suspect them. However, Shakespeare seizes the chance for some amusing satire and draws a caricature of the *affected fop,* the *empty-headed* fashionable gallant of the court, wearing much of his estate on his back and head, in silks and plumes. Osric is a parallel to many characters in books of verse satire and in satiric comedies by Ben Jonson and others.

MINOR CHARACTERS: The remainder of the cast serve almost entirely for obvious minor functions of plot. It might be remarked that Marcellus, Bernardo, and Francisco speak to one another and to Horatio as equals, that is, gentlemen (compare I.2.196). One would infer, then, that they are officers, though perhaps of lower rank; and their standing on guard is perhaps not usual military practice. But Shakespeare avoids any mention of rank; he wants men in that night-scene who can talk easily to the scholar Horatio about affairs in Denmark, for this is the necessary *exposition* of the play. So the dramatist counts on the audience's not noticing or caring about a minor violation of realism.

A Commentary on the Action

Act I

SCENE 1. Most editions tell us that the setting is "a platform" before the castle. Certainly this does not mean a floor raised on scaffolding. In fact, at the Globe Theater the audience, knowing the play to be *Hamlet* and seeing a sentinel at his post, would assume he was stationed in the area before the castle gates or castle doors, and so indeed he is.[1]

Traditionally, *Hamlet* begins with twelve slow strokes of a bell backstage, to bring the audience to close attention and to signify the time as midnight. The twelve strokes are prolonged and slow enough to create suspense.

As Francisco, the sentinel, paces across the stage, Bernardo, his successor, enters at some distance behind him, peering about in the imaginary darkness, with obvious nervousness. Bernardo perceives the shadowy figure moving before him and challenges it, rather than waiting to be challenged, as one might expect a soldier to do. Francisco whirls around and with responsive nervousness cries, *Nay, YOU answer ME!* Bernardo gives the password. Francisco, chilled by the nipping air of midnight and dreading a danger he only senses, is glad to leave the watch to Bernardo and his two companions for this night, Marcellus and Horatio. Horatio, Marcellus, and Bernardo seem to be gentlemen much of the same class, Marcellus and Bernardo probably being lieutenants or ensigns. Horatio has been a university student, not an army man. Military and civilian costumes at once reveal some of these relations.

The audience's curiosity, aroused by the bell beats and the anxiety of the sentries, is heightened and directed by the question, *What* ['Well'], *has this thing appeared again tonight?* Knowing the story, the audience realizes the point at which the play is beginning—the appearance of the Ghost! The short conversation which follows just allows time for this thrilling idea to sink in before the spectre itself appears. But the brief talk also tells them that Horatio is a skeptic about ghosts, and that he is here to find out its nature, if indeed it is not just hallucination. (Beyond any question, Shakespeare represents the Ghost as some kind of spiritual reality; for it is seen by four persons, one of them a man of intellectual quality. It is an actual being.)

There is a bench, probably well downstage (toward the front), and the talkers have seated themselves on it (33), facing the audience, but glancing now and then at a stage door opposite to that at which they entered. Suddenly a stately figure fills the opposite doorway, a being in full armor, with the visor of his helmet raised (62; also, I.3.200, 229). His face is pale and frowning. He carries a marshal's baton (I.2.204). The three young men are visibly shaken *with fear and wonder* (44); the scoffer, Horatio, makes no move to leave his companions and confront the Ghost as it strides in slow, but military, dignity, across the stage toward the door by which they entered. But prompted by his companions, Horatio in a shaking voice calls, "What spirit are you that have taken this form of Denmark's dead king?" With only a glance at him, the Ghost walks slowly out the door, as if moving into the courtyard of the palace in search of someone.

Horatio, pale and trembling, testifies to the reality of the spirit. The long conversation that follows before the return of the Ghost serves a number of purposes for the drama: (1) It builds suspense for the Ghost's return; (2) it states the thematic idea that the apparition prophesies *some strange eruption* (or *fierce events*) for Denmark (68, 121), and indeed these are to be manifest in the deaths of Hamlet, Gertrude, and Claudius; and (3) it gives in full the background of Fortinbras, father and son, as foils to Hamlet, father and son. Someone, perhaps the Lord Chamberlain's Men, cut this speech short, finding that it dulled anticipation of the Ghost's reappearance.[2] It is interesting that in this conversation Horatio becomes to some degree a chorus character, an interpreter of events to follow, as well as primarily an expositor of needed information.

It is important to grasp the dramatic significance of both the elder and younger Fortinbras. Though not a king, Fortinbras the father was a nobleman possessed of great estates and power in Norway and was even a distant kinsman of King Hamlet of Denmark (V.2.399-401). In spite of this relationship, perhaps even *because* of it, Fortinbras challenged King Hamlet to single combat, sending him a formal cartel in which the stakes were named —all of Fortinbras's land-holdings! Though in return King Hamlet was to wager an equal extent of his lands, his risk was not quite so great, for his kingdom was larger than Fortinbras's earldom, and if defeated, the King would have something left. Obviously, Fortinbras possessed great daring. Probably the weapons and the place of combat were to be chosen by King Hamlet, the defender (Horatio's language suggests that Renaissance practice is to be understood). King Hamlet not only defeated his challenger, but killed him—not necessarily by intent, of course; to disarm or injure his adversary would have sufficed to win the contest, in terms of the Italian *duello*. But the whole episode (though not the words that are used) is surely drawn from a Scandinavian custom, the *holmgang* of the heroic age. The Hamlet story was first a Norse saga.

Think of young Fortinbras's situation now that he has reached manhood. Without property or living, with much diminished honor and a tarnished name, the youth also possesses his father's proud nature. He is desperate; he must do something to reinstate himself. Keeping a distance from the capital of Norway in order to avoid the notice of his king, he quickly gathers up a company of younger sons without estates, luckless gentlemen out of positions, professional adventurers—not riffraff, but men with a disposition for making a profit by fighting. With this battalion of desperates Fortinbras seems to be planning an invasion of the earldom his father lost (some of it may adjoin Denmark itself) while Claudius, the new king, is still settling himself on the throne of Denmark. Once in possession, Fortinbras will probably be able to retain most of his lost estates. But Claudius is vigorously preparing to prevent this strategy.

Let us return to the watchers at Elsinore. Now it is Horatio, his spirits somewhat quieted by the talk, who first notices the Ghost's re-entry as it is about to cross the stage on its way to its sepulchre. It will leave by the door where it first entered; and Horatio, seeing this intention (*Lo, where it comes {back} again!*) realizes he must stop it now or not at all. He resolves to cross its path—a great risk; for if this apparition is a devil, to cross it is to seek contact with it and its deadly power. But Horatio crosses, going upstage and turning around to face the audience, as he four times exhorts it to speak.[3] In addressing the Ghost, Horatio names three traditional reasons for spirits' haunting their old places: (1) to induce someone to perform a duty that the spirit left undone while in its mortal life (Horatio offers to perform the duty and thus gain grace from Heaven for his charity, 131); (2) to warn his countrymen of some disaster that is coming; and (3) to reveal to his friends a hoard of ill-gotten money, so that it may be distributed to his creditors or to the poor.

The Ghost pauses for a moment and raises its downcast face to look at Horatio as if about to answer him (I.215-217); but just then, backstage, as from a distant farm, sounds the crowing of a cock. The Ghost drops its half-raised arm, turns abruptly, and somewhat more rapidly strides to the door of its first entrance. Marcellus and Bernardo make half-hearted efforts to overtake it; yet, if Marcellus extends his partisan (spear) to bar the way, he takes care to stay so far to the side that he is in no real danger of interfering with the Ghost's exit, and Bernardo stands safely behind him and echoes his cry. These maneuvers are somewhat humorous, but they need not turn the scene into a farcical chase. Shakespeare has sufficiently emphasized the awe of the Ghost's appearances.

The men pause for a rather long discussion of the effect of cockcrow upon spirits. Doubtless this talk is a modulation, dramatically, toward the council scene that follows; or the discussion releases the tension of the Ghost's appearance. To have the trumpets blare the flourish for the council just after the Ghost's exit would not properly prepare for the importance of that scene. But incidentally, note that the ambiguity about the Ghost's nature is developed by the restatement of folk-ideas about fairies, witches, wandering spirits. The walkers of the night cannot abide God's sunshine, which is heralded by the cockcrow before dawn (about three o'clock). And the present scene has lasted about three hours of stage time.

SCENE 2. As the trumpets shrill out the bars of a flourish, which is the musical signal for the entrance or exit of the sovereign, stage attendants quickly open the curtains on the rear alcove or door and bring on the *state,* the throne (and at the same time remove the bench used in Scene 1). They place the throne just in front of the rear stage wall; beside the throne they place a large chair for the Queen. A procession enters from the right: an usher leading King Claudius, Queen Gertrude, Polonius, Laertes, Ophelia, several lords, and a lady-in-waiting to the Queen. Lagging near the end is Hamlet, dressed entirely in black, which contrasts with the brilliant colors worn by the other characters; his slower pace and gloomy manner re-enforce this contrast.[4] Claudius and Gertrude seat themselves; Polonius and his children stand respectfully (facing the audience) at Claudius's side; Hamlet and the lords and lady group themselves at Gertrude's side; and thus Claudius's first meeting of state with his court is ready to

A Commentary on the Action / Act I

begin. The scene has begun very ceremoniously because it is like a union of two state occasions, the King's address from the throne at the opening of Parliament and a meeting of the King with his Privy Council to consider policy in an emergency. The governing class of the kingdom are here represented by Polonius, chief councilor, and the lords attendant.

Claudius's address from the throne begins in quite formal language, for it must at first deal with two somewhat delicate subjects, his immediate marriage to his brother's widow (it is less than two months since King Hamlet died, 138) and his immediate accession to the throne after his brother's sudden death. In the presence of Hamlet, the bereaved son and heir, the least possible mention of these topics will be best. Underlying Claudius's guarded, brief statement is the implication that the safety of the nation impelled him to these rapid actions (*discretion* [prudence for his country] *fought with nature* [grief for his dead brother]). Patriotism, then, urged him to join his masculine intelligence and firmness, as well as his royal blood, to Gertrude's actual possession of sovereignty, in order to meet the threat from young Fortinbras's preparations.

Let us stop to describe the political constitution of Denmark, for of course it is part of the complexity of Hamlet's whole situation. But the term *constitution* implies a definiteness which is not really present in this aspect of the play. We have to infer that Shakespeare thought the Danish monarchy was elective, with this restriction, that aspirants to sovereignty must have some kinship to the royal family (young Fortinbras seems to base his claim on blood relationship, V.2.400-401). Hamlet had *hopes* of election, strong ones, we should expect (V.2.64-65), for he was the natural heir, and he was of age. But Claudius *popped in,* instead. How? Claudius's gratitude to Polonius, expressed in this scene (45-49), and his dependence on the old man later strongly suggest that Polonius was able to lead a large enough faction among the electing nobility in support of Claudius, to overrule those who favored young Hamlet, who was attending the University of Wittenberg at the time of his father's unexpected death. Probably the audience supposed that about four days' time was needed to carry the word to Hamlet at Wittenberg and bring him back to Elsinore, and that that was time enough for Claudius's intrigue to achieve success. Nearly prostrated with grief at the loss of his father[5] and horrified at his mother's decision to remarry at once, Hamlet was not prepared to rally support for a rebellion against Claudius's *coup d'état*. And Claudius was mustering the nation against Fortinbras (I.1.104-107); to oppose him would be to appear unpatriotic.

Let us return to the action of Scene 2. In brief, decisive terms Claudius directs his warning to the old King of Norway. The firm manner in which Claudius is handling the crisis arouses our respect, even though, like the Globe audience, we know the Hamlet-story and are aware Claudius is the murderer of his brother. Doubtless Shakespeare intended to contrast the King to the mentally sick and vacillating young Hamlet; but allowing for that effect, we should not be unduly influenced in Claudius's favor. Malignant criminals may often show qualities of intelligence and firmness, but their natures are not less evil because of them. Certainly Claudius will prove a powerful antagonist for the hero.

When Voltimand and Cornelius have gone on their embassy, Claudius shows another aspect of his character, his geniality to those who may be useful to him or (let us give him all credit possible) those whom he likes. But some critics find his manner to Laertes and other friends too effusive, insistent, or oily. Even if it is sincere, his manner has a politician's heartiness. Yet he is too intelligent ever to lapse into mere emotionalism. Note how carefully he sounds out the father's opinion before giving permission for Laertes to sow some wild oats in France,[6] and how quickly he then turns to his discontented nephew.

We can interpret Claudius's relation to Hamlet correctly here, only if we realize that Hamlet's manner clearly reveals the dominance of melancholy over him, and Claudius's consequent uneasiness and frustration in dealing with him. Let us review the causes which, as the Elizabethans see Hamlet's situation, have plunged the Prince into mental disease deep enough to prompt him to suicide (131-132), though he has apparently retained his rationality and most of his judgment. The causes are: (1) the unexpected death of a father whom he has idolized (at least he believes he loved him thus); (2) the discovery that his mother has not loved her husband as she seemed to; (3) the discovery that his mother is a very sensual woman who has to marry again within two months of her husband's death; (4) Hamlet's shame because the publicity of her marriage necessarily reveals her sensuality and callousness to all Denmark; (5) his mother's marriage to a man whom the prince has always instinctively disliked (I.5.40-41); (6) the loss of the throne to this despised uncle; and (7) Hamlet's having no political forces adequate to reverse Claudius's *coup d'état*. There are probably other irksome

A Commentary on the Action / Act I

things in his situation which you can name, but these seven are more than enough to explain a profoundly bad mental state.

Let us emphasize the importance of (6). Hamlet, like any young prince, has been brought up for a career as governor of his people. This high function and responsibility have always been his goal and ideal. Suddenly its achievement is removed far into the future (if it will materialize at all); for certainly Claudius is in younger middle-age and may live many years. Of course, King Hamlet might have been expected to live a considerable time, also; but under him the Prince would have gradually assumed many military and civil responsibilities in a natural way. Even if King Claudius were not now a man with a guilty conscience, he and Hamlet must necessarily be suspicious of each other, and Hamlet in consequence must be a lonely man without genuine function in the life of Denmark.

Looking to such a future, therefore, Hamlet is already a deeply melancholy man, a fact manifested to the audience by the manner of his entrance and by his costume. In fact, he is in a general fashion the *malcontent* (or "discontented") man, a stage type quite familiar then. How can he not be an *ambitious* man—an aspirant to the power which he can only achieve by violence against the sovereign? His being the victim of Claudius's intrigue of course brings him sympathy. But in stage tradition his posture, costume, and blunt, disrespectful answers sound the usual overtones of menace and moral ambiguity in the malcontent figure, a revengeful victim of injustice.

Claudius addresses Hamlet as *my cousin and my son*—cousin signifying, as usual, an indefinite blood relationship not so close as child or sibling. Claudius probably intends the word to be a polite evasion of the specific *nephew,* which too strongly bespeaks the incest of the marriage; but to mention any other relation than the new sonship was tactless and, therefore, in some degree stupid. It arouses Hamlet's scorn. As Claudius turns with an unctuous smile to his new bride, who returns the smile uneasily, Hamlet bitterly growls to the audience, [*By this marriage I am*] *a little more than* [*blood*] *kin* [*to this fellow,*] *and* [*yet, despite this closeness, my feelings are*] *less than kind.* But Hamlet also puns on *kind* meaning 'natural'; Claudius is *less than kind,* for incest is unnatural.[7] Hamlet's first words are characteristically witty and ironic.

After his rude reply to Claudius's reproachful question (66), Gertrude remonstrates with Hamlet against his unfriendliness to the new stepfather, as evidenced by his wearing of mourning during the wedding festivities and by his short answers. Hamlet's emphatic reply has a note of anger and sharp irony; in *his* mourning there is no dissimulation, as there has been in hers and Claudius's. Claudius now tries to reason firmly with the young man, on grounds of Christian morality and Stoic impassivity, that such a prolonged and deep mourning is unmanly and sinful. We note in his remarks no reference at all to his personal grief for a dead brother. Naturally, neither Claudius nor Gertrude alludes to any other cause for Hamlet's melancholy than sorrow; but the other causes are in their minds. Claudius ends by an explicit proffer of friendship: "Let me be, as I wish, your loving father." But belief in his sincerity is hardly possible here; for without stopping, he immediately denies Hamlet's request to go back to the university. Why? He cannot allow a malcontent young enemy to go to a distant place where he might, undetected, prepare an attack on Claudius.

Hamlet's silent, bitter look after Claudius's long speech doubtless shows his comprehension of Claudius's motives. But Claudius must publicly interpret this hostility for the best; and besides, he is a drunkard. So he calls Hamlet's submission a *gentle and unforc'd accord* and decides to make it the excuse for a carouse. At least he has prevailed without an angry dispute with the Prince.

As the trumpets play the flourish, the Council ends, and Hamlet is left to consider the empty throne and his own miserable condition. He speaks the first of four major soliloquies in this play. They are eloquent, but not always clear, expressions of his spiritual distress and intellectual groping for a true conception of his own motives and obligations.

This first soliloquy, however, is simpler than those that follow. It is primarily a statement for the audience of the mental symptoms of melancholia which has progressed to the point of a hatred of living (129-132). For Hamlet there is nothing in the world (at least the world of men) which is not either futile (133) or foul (136). The words *stale, rank, gross,* with their suggestions of stench, prepare the imagination for the sudden revelation of Hamlet's fundamental source of disgust, his mother's shocking sensuality, which has driven her within two months to drop all pretense of grieving and to marry a notorious sensualist, her brother-in-law. It is a torment to Hamlet to remember how she formerly fondled and caressed his father; those caresses, he now sees, meant, not spiritual love, but mere lust. To Hamlet, her

A Commentary on the Action / Act I

hypocrisy deepens her guilt. The fact that her second marriage is incestuous still further blackens her character and shames her son. Let us stop to note that in the theology of the Anglican Church, as of the Catholic Church, the sacraments of Baptism and Matrimony created spiritual relationships which were almost as strong as those of blood kinship. For instance, Gertrude's marriage to King Hamlet established a spiritual relation with Claudius which precluded marriage if King Hamlet should die. How Claudius and Gertrude managed to be married by the Church the play does not tell; but that they obtained some kind of dispensation and were married is clear; for the Council of State approved the union (14-16, above). Presumably the Council would not have approved if the Church had continued to refuse the permission. But Hamlet disregards this legalizing as merely a bowing to Claudius's power. For Hamlet the marriage is an offense to God and man, and it remains so (V.2.336) to the end.

The superlative terms in which Hamlet speaks of his father, calling him Hyperion and Hercules, have suggested to modern readers adept in psychology that in this play Shakespeare was dealing in Freudian ideas, though without the psychological language of today. (Hyperion was one of the pre-Olympian gods, a Titan; Hercules was notable for his sexuality.) In other words, Hamlet may appear, in his idolatry of his father, to be reacting against a former infantile father-hatred, founded on an infantile sexual love of his mother. Does he suffer from an Oedipus complex and, having subconsciously hated his father, does he now suppress the guilty feeling by fiercely idolizing the dead man? However, it has also been proposed that Hamlet's present psychoneurotic state began, rather, in an unconscious homosexual love of his father; he is an "Oedipus Opposite." Now that the father is dead, the feeling which before had been repressed comes into the open, and the hatred of his rival, his mother, and also his loathing of heterosexual love become more overt.

For either of these views certain elements in the play offer objections. Against the first it may be urged that the play gives no evidence that Hamlet had betrayed hatred of his father in earlier life; and his hatred of Claudius has genuine non-sexual foundations even without the fact of murder. Against the second it may be urged that Hamlet's relations with Ophelia before the appearance of the Ghost and Hamlet's character in general do not suggest a homosexual character. Yet it must be admitted that Hamlet's sex-loathing appears so strong as to justify an attempt to interpret it in Freudian terms. However, great caution is to be used in so doing, for: (1) Any artist before the twentieth century who appears to be dealing in Freudian motifs must be doing so intuitively and, from our point of view, incompletely (in fact, depth psychology is still a relatively young and undeveloped science). (2) It is probable that to Shakespeare and his audience Hamlet's motives and behavior were much clearer than to us, in fact, quite satisfactorily clear—simply because certain implications and niceties of story, staging, and language have been lost to us and not yet recovered, but were understood by Elizabethans. Therefore, it is our obligation to do our utmost to understand *Hamlet* in Elizabethan terms before we rely on modern theories of personality.

Let us return, once more, to Scene 2. Hamlet ends his first soliloquy in tears of grief and shame, so that when Horatio, Marcellus, and Bernardo enter to greet him, he does not at first recognize them and turns aside his face while wiping away the tears (160-161). But then recognizing his friend, he clasps his hand with enthusiasm and greets the others warmly. He listens with wonder and passionate anticipation to the description of the Ghost (which we have utilized in commenting on Scene 1). He wonders about the Ghost's purpose—can his father be angry at Gertrude's faithlessness? But no, says Horatio, it was sorrowful and pale. So its purpose remains mysterious.

When he dismisses the young men, Hamlet corrects their greeting, *duty to your honour,* by saying, "Your *love,* please—in return for mine to you." This friendliness and eagerness for love is a facet of the prince's character not to be forgotten. Though melancholiac and despondent, the kind, responsive youth is still to be felt in him (and it will also be implied in his relations with Rosencrantz and Guildenstern).

The short soliloquy at the end of the scene (255-258) only expresses Hamlet's feeling that *he is in danger from Claudius.* He has no suspicion of his father's murder. In line 256, *foul play* means (as regularly in other dramas) 'ugly plot, underhanded trickery.'[8] But Hamlet thinks the Ghost may wish to warn him of a plot against his own life. (For Hamlet's surprise when he learns of his father's murder, see I.5.25-26.)

SCENE 3. Scene 2 must have ended near mid-day (see I.1.174-175). To prevent Hamlet's midnight encounter with the Ghost from following too awkwardly soon after the Prince's parting from

A Commentary on the Action / Act I

Horatio and Marcellus, Shakespeare inserts Scene 3. But Scene 3 also serves to introduce a group of minor characters whose lives are fatally, yet ironically, bound up with Hamlet's disaster. Polonius and his children all die as a result of Hamlet's spasmodic attempts to extricate himself from evil; but despite their tragedy, these three persons create a good deal of ironic humor.

Note the ironies in Scene 3: (1) The wind is favorable, the vessel is waiting, (as both father and son emphasize), yet eighty-five lines are required for Laertes to bid farewell to sister and father—even though he has once already bid farewell to his father and is now concluding his farewell to his sister. This delay is due to two long moral discourses, one from brother to sister, the other (as if in punishment) from father to son. (2) In fact, we see here a case of "like father, like son." A sign of Polonius's senility is his garrulousness and egotism; the symptoms of this incipient trouble are to be seen in Laertes. So the son's pompous lecture to his sister seems appropriately answered by the father's heavy array of maxims. Whether Laertes perceives his resemblance to his father is doubtful. But there is little doubt that Ophelia perceives a third irony in the scene: (3) the absurdity of Laertes's lecturing her about being a good girl at home when he is about to go off to enjoy himself in Paris. To the Elizabethans a young man's sojourn in Paris for a year or so meant just about what such an experience represents to our minds. It is perfectly clear that neither Polonius nor Laertes supposes that the young man will spend months studying in the Louvre or the Bibliothèque Nationale.

Ophelia cuts off Laertes's sermon with a reference to the *primrose path of dalliance* he certainly will trace. *O fear me not. I stay* [delay] *too long,* he replies hastily. As he asks Polonius for the second farewell blessing, Laertes kneels on one knee; and he is kept in this uncomfortable position (unless he shifts to two knees) through twenty-seven lines of precepts. (Line 81 seems to end the blessing.) There has been sharp difference of opinion as to the respect we should pay to Polonius's advice to Laertes (58-81). Although, taken out of context, many of the maxims are quite sound pieces of practical instruction, taken as a whole we have to say that they tell a young man how to *make a good impression* and *avoid expensive blunders,* especially when he is among strangers. To get ahead in the world is understood as the goal; Polonius makes no reference at all to ideals, duty, devotion to country or class, or keeping a clear conscience before God. The homily ends with the maxim, *to thine own self be true,/And ... /Thou canst not then be false to any man.* This seems to recommend the highest chivalric sense of honor. But, ambiguously, it may only mean, "Keep your own success always in view, and then you will not betray anyone else, for treachery is too risky."[9]

When at last Laertes can stiffly arise and go, he cautions Ophelia to remember his warning; Ophelia promises to speak of it to no one, but her father's senile curiosity is aroused, and she must at once half reveal Laertes's concern. Polonius has had this matter on his mind too; in fact, he says that someone *put it on him* by way of caution, his phrase suggesting that either Claudius or Gertrude has warned him of danger in Hamlet's attention to Ophelia. Since, later on, Gertrude twice says she had hoped Hamlet would marry Ophelia (III.1.37-42; V.1.267), it is unlikely that Shakespeare intended the audience even momentarily to think of Gertrude as opposed to such a marriage.

Presumably, then, Claudius warned Polonius to beware of bad results from Hamlet's wooing of Ophelia. What results? If we take Claudius's view, possibly a marriage between Hamlet and Ophelia might lead to better mental health in the prince,[10] and if it did, this recovery, coupled with a strong bond between Polonius and Hamlet, potentially would create a faction zealous to put Hamlet on the throne (birth of a son to Hamlet and Ophelia would intensify this danger). A melancholy prince is more subject to Claudius's control, being a sick man. But we should not expect Claudius to say all this to Polonius; rather, he might say, "The melancholy Hamlet has lost rational control of his behavior. Beware of what may happen to Ophelia." It is true that Polonius does not mention melancholy as the cause of untrustworthiness in Hamlet; like Laertes, he talks of the danger of passion overruling the restraints of conscience or honor. Laertes believes that for political reasons Hamlet cannot marry Ophelia, and their love affair, if continued, can end only in disgrace for her. Polonius does not speak of the political aspect.[11] That he should ignore it, as well as Hamlet's melancholy, perhaps may be explained on the ground that for the immediate purpose of the story, it is necessary for Polonius to separate the lovers without calculating the political advantages to himself that might result from his fostering it.

Anyway, it is certain that Polonius's command to Ophelia does produce the plot effect which is needed; and it is also certain that the dramatist knew the audience would *not* weigh the probabilities as we have tried to weigh them in the preceding paragraph.

A Commentary on the Action / Act I

It is likely that they accepted without careful analysis this episode of the familiar story, and if the obscure warning (from Claudius?) produced any reaction, it was no more than the audience's half-conscious recognition of another sign of political villainy.[12]

Without making any protest, Ophelia accepts Polonius's command to break off her relations with Hamlet. We may soften our contempt for her submissiveness by remembering the duty of strict obedience to parental authority—universally preached, though not universally observed—and also the fact that Hamlet should properly marry a princess. But nothing can much affect our belief that by nature Ophelia lacks a normal human determination and courage to oppose injustice to herself and her lover. We are left with the question why Shakespeare makes her so unheroic. Probably a major reason is his intention to leave Hamlet all the more alone, without any serious rival for the audience's interest. Her abandonment of Hamlet also plunges the hero deeper into melancholy, as is fully apparent in II.1.

SCENE 4. In Scene 3 Polonius has prepared more misery for Hamlet; and now the play returns to its major theme, the Ghost and its revelation. Hamlet, Horatio, and Marcellus at once alert the audience to expect a second apparition by their apprehensive talk of the biting cold and the late hour. But this second scene of awaiting the Ghost has a new counterpoint to deepen its significance for Hamlet, that is, the occasional distant music of horns and boom of cannon. The fact that cannon shooting also served as a device for thunder in the Globe Theater may also prepare for a supernatural visitation; for thunder and the supernatural have ancient, strong associations. But more important, the cannon-shots symbolize Claudius's triumphant possession of a throne that is rightfully Hamlet's; they are like a hateful taunting of the prince. And again they enforce a contrast between the lecherous, drunken murderer and the heroic brother whose Ghost presently comes to demand punishment of the villain.

Hamlet's long speech is probably intended to increase suspense; for its involved sentence structure and wordiness add up to a fairly simple idea which Shakespeare could have put in more compact form, had he not wished to suggest that Hamlet's mind was wandering from his subject to the expected appearance of the Ghost.[13] And presently the spirit comes, probably from the same door as in Scene 1. If it enters with downcast face, at Horatio's exclamation (38) it raises its head; and Hamlet, like his friends, is deeply moved by its countenance revealing more of sorrow than of anger. But of course Hamlet's doubt remains—is this truly the spirit of his dead father (whether in or out of its body) or is it a devil which has taken possession of the body or is merely deceiving the men's senses with an illusion? Hamlet's first words, then, are a very significant prayer for protection against diabolical powers. The most important function of the Heavenly angels is their protection of mankind against the intellectual and spiritual assaults of devils. This fatherly-looking being now gazing at Hamlet may be Satan himself.

However, as Hamlet says, it comes in *questionable shape,* that is, in a familiar instead of terrifying appearance. He asks, in solemn language that reveals his awe, why the dead man returned and what should be done to procure it rest. But the fatal command to revenge (along with the news of Claudius's guilt) is to be heard by Hamlet alone, and so the Ghost only beckons the Prince to follow back through the door by which the Ghost has just entered.

The strenuous objections by Hamlet's companions indicate that Hamlet's decision to follow the Ghost is more important than we might at first think. In the ages which believed completely in the constant efforts of the devil and his angels to seduce the human soul moment by moment throughout life, any least consent to the devil's will might in itself be damnable or quickly lead to damnable yielding. This is why Horatio implies that even the consent to go to another place, if it were followed at once by death without time for repentance, would result in Hamlet's damnation. Of course the idea is just as familiar to Hamlet as to Horatio; this is why Hamlet's words

> I do not set my life at a pin's fee,
> And for my soul, what can it do to that,
> Being a thing immortal as itself? (65-67)

sin by rashness—a presumption either that Hamlet is able of his own power to overcome the devil's strength or that God will furnish protection even if Hamlet *deliberately* accepts a diabolical temptation. However, the words also impress us with the Prince's courage and faith in the truth of the Ghost's being his father's spirit. Note line 81, *My fate cries out;* Hamlet seems to sense that the Ghost's appearance is in some way a work of Providence or destiny.

When he has gone, Horatio and Marcellus pause, nervously

A Commentary on the Action / Act I

uncertain whether to obey Hamlet's fierce gesture (*I say, away!*) or to follow. Their short exchange allows time for the Ghost and Hamlet to disappear (as we imagine) behind some corner of the castle wall or in the shadows of an adjoining building.

SCENE 5. There seems no good reason for believing this was played as an interior scene. If it were done in an "inner stage" or house of some kind, not only would the actors be much less visible to the audience, but they would be put into a nearness to each other which would diminish the dramatic effect. Rather, after Horatio and Marcellus have followed the other pair off stage through the Ghost's usual door, Hamlet and the Ghost return to the outer stage through another door; for the conventional way of showing a change of location was to exit and re-enter another way. Perhaps they return through the inner stage, but walk to the outer stage. The Ghost moves a little to one side; Hamlet stops and possibly leans against one of the pillars of the "Heavens." He will need this support in a few moments.

Hamlet's interview with the Ghost raises some of the most fundamental and abstruse difficulties in this complex tragedy. In fact, for some critics, the answer to the question, What are the nature and authority of the Ghost? gives us direction for understanding the whole of Hamlet's disaster.[14] But after all the innumerable studies of this play, there is still sharp disagreement about how Shakespeare intended the audience to interpret the Ghost, and the questions dependent on that understanding are therefore not wholly settled.

There are at least three alternative views, probably more: (1) The Ghost is a Senecan Ghost, in dramatic terms an impersonation of the impulse to revenge, and therefore essentially of the impulses of pride and anger, which are evil passions, sources of crime and misery. (2) The Ghost is a Christian soul released from Purgatory by the will of God to impose on Hamlet the duty of removing from the throne of Denmark a moral monster, who has thrust himself into the position of God's vice-gerent. (3) The Ghost is a dramatic convention, a kind of amalgam of (1) and (2) and of folk-lore about wandering spirits; as such, it is morally ambiguous (because it is spiritually ambiguous).[15]

The less common view that the Ghost is an apparition of Satan to delude Hamlet into murder is morally very close to (1). To each of these interpretations there are serious objections. For instance, to the first, there is the objection that the Ghost describes his punishment as if he were a soul in Purgatory (9-13). To the second, it is objected that the Ghost calls for revenge, and apparently with quite a personal vindictiveness. Against the third, we may say that a Senecan Ghost and a Christian Ghost are essentially different in moral quality and cannot be combined as a dramatic idea.[16]

Nearly everyone accepts as true that the Ghost speaks as if he dwells in the penal region of Purgatory, whose existence is an article of Catholic faith. His punishment is twofold, in daylight hours to agonize in fires like those of Hell itself (this is the orthodox conception of Purgatory) and also, during the night, to walk without rest through the places of his earthly life (a punishment more common in folklore than in theological description). Neither punishment signifies that King Hamlet has committed great *crimes;* in line 12 the word has the Latin sense of "faults." But what the world calls "ordinary sins" may, as offenses against infinite Goodness and Justice, demand years of punishment. This use of the doctrine of Purgatory in Elizabethan, Protestant London is undeniably surprising; but we may note that to have the Ghost come from either Hell or Heaven would have been far more incredible, as presenting either a demonic lost soul which hates God, Claudius, and Gertrude alike, or on the other hand, a soul in bliss, free of all resentment against Claudius or protectiveness for Gertrude.

Although God's choice of a human soul to bring a command to Hamlet can be supported by authority in scholastic philosophy and by the Biblical example of Samuel, the idea is contrary to Protestant theology. However, it is fit that the father should incite the son to an act of personal and national justice, and that the former King should call for the removal from the throne of Denmark of a murderer and incestuous adulterer. Because of this appropriateness and because the tradition of revenge tragedy often made use of a ghost to instigate the revenge, Shakespeare uses the Ghost of King Hamlet. Note carefully two aspects of the Ghost—he speaks with a powerful personal feeling which compels the audience's sympathy with his resentment, shame, and horror; and yet his recital is apparently controlled by a moral viewpoint that seems founded on justice and purity. He does not rage against Claudius as if the infliction of pain on his betrayer were his object. The just punishment of crime appears the supernatural motive of this commission to the Prince. So strong is one's impression of this high moral purpose that lines 84-85 have pro-

A Commentary on the Action / Act I

voked a good deal of discussion. Whether the Ghost means "Do not suspect your mother of any part in the murder" or "Do not give way to feelings of hate as you prepare to kill Claudius," perhaps we cannot be sure;[17] but either way the Ghost is urging Hamlet to avoid passion, to be judicial. If the Ghost were a devil, the lines would be incongruous. True, the word *revenge* is used in 7, 25, and 31. But in Elizabethan English the word is often equivalent to *avenge,* that is, 'punish.' The Lord punishes, at times, through human instruments.

Let us now consider the effect of the Ghost's revelations on the melancholy Hamlet—for he has been suicidally melancholy, as we have seen. What does he learn from the Ghost that will be agonizing to a mind already so ill? (1) That his father has been murdered—cut off in the prime of life; (2) that his mother's corruption has been so deep that she betrayed her husband and turned to incestuous adultery; (3) that she and Claudius played hypocrites in pretending fondness for King Hamlet; (4) that his father must suffer hellish torments for a long time because of Claudius's treachery; and (5) that he himself is appointed, inescapably, to kill the reigning King of Denmark, if possible, in such a way as to extract from the dying man a confession of the murder—but without revealing Gertrude's adultery. In view of the horror of these revelations and the difficulties in number (5), we shall not be surprised to find Hamlet near madness at the beginning of Act II.

We have already noted that Hamlet has not suspected the murder (see the comment on the end of Scene 2, above). His surprise is expressed in line 26, in which there are four silent metrical feet, a long pause in which Hamlet expresses his amazement by posture and expression. The irony of his proposal to hasten to the act of murder (29-31) is almost hilarious, considering the universal conception of him as the delaying Hamlet. The words are spoken in a first rush of anger, which we know, ironically, cannot survive the horrific revelations that are to follow. Hamlet's *O my prophetic soul!* (40-41) has to be understood only as expressing his recollection of always detesting his uncle without knowing why. If Hamlet has had suspicion of his father's dying by unnatural means (not to speak of suspecting Claudius to be the agent) the first soliloquy, I.2.129-159, should have revealed it.

The impact of the discovery of the murder is great enough, but even greater is their mutual shame and anguish as the Ghost recites Gertrude's treachery. Hamlet covers his face and is silent.[18] The Ghost's words grow more rapid, for he senses the approach of daylight; and finally, with a gesture of farewell, he turns and slowly exits by a side door. Hamlet is alone, and nearly hysterical. He begins to swear his eternal devotion to his father by heaven, earth, and hell—but the last word seems shameful (*O, fie!*) because of his father's punishment. To relieve his tormented mind he takes from his pocket his ivory tablets (107) and tries to write down a new "sentence" (apothegm) he has learned (108) and below that, his motto (*word* 110). Offstage center are heard the calls of Horatio and Marcellus, and presently the men enter through the center door, as Hamlet and the Ghost did.

Hamlet greets them with silly talk. His mind is truly near madness in this scene; the burden of the Ghost's revelations strains Hamlet's reason near to cracking. Let us not forget, also, that he cannot possibly reveal so soon what he has learned even to Horatio—and anyway, Marcellus is present. Too distracted to contrive any evasion, he can only plead with them to believe it is indeed the Ghost of his father and to suppress their curiosity about its message. Hamlet realizes his need for absolute secrecy and so asks them to swear it. They swear *on their faith* (145-146), but this is too trivial an oath; they might forget it or discount it. So he holds out the hilt of his sword, which makes a cross, and they place their hands on it. This silent gesture constitutes the oath, given three times, at 155, 160, and 181. The deep voice of the Ghost crying *Swear!* from understage (the traditional "Hell" of the theater), the nervousness of the friends, as they trail about the stage, and Hamlet's language of contemptuous familiarity to the spirit make a scene of such grotesque humor that no spectator could ever forget it.

In fact, the humor of the scene is so near to farce that to a reader it seems hard to defend. However, we remember that Shakespeare's presentation of the Ghost has been extremely naturalistic with respect to the surroundings, the behavior of the persons involved, and the temperament of the spirit himself. To introduce the supernatural there were no thunderclaps or infernal fire and smoke; and Hamlet did not respond to the revelations about Claudius with any heroical rant. In a sense, the grotesque epithets he applies to the Ghost during the swearing on the sword are further evidence of the hysterical excitement in which he parted from the Ghost, and are to that degree natural. But the threefold repetition in different parts of the stage, and the

A Commentary on the Action / Act I

underground voice of the Ghost as prompter cannot easily be justified as naturalism. It seems very likely that this stage business was a popular part of the old *Hamlet* play that Shakespeare did not feel free to discard. Those who interpret the Ghost as an evil being have pointed to this episode as proof, for the Ghost cries from "Hell" (the understage), and Hamlet addresses him as if he were a familiar devil, in a tone resembling that of medieval drama. To the present writer the episode offers no distinct evidence of the Ghost's being a demon. Note the farewell, *Rest, rest, perturbed spirit* (182).

And now Hamlet prepares his friends (and the audience) for his *antic disposition* (172). In short, it is to be his "assumed madness." But it is always to be carefully distinguished from the symptoms of melancholia, such as self-blame, wish for death, rationalizing, which he expresses in soliloquy or with Horatio, and also from moments of near-hysteria such as the present one or that after "The Mouse-Trap." The antic disposition is made up of those words and actions which Hamlet uses to make people believe his mind has been made irrational by melancholy, and he uses the traditional signs for illness. Among them are *extreme rudeness* to persons deserving of respect, for example, Claudius, Polonius, Gertrude, Ophelia, Rosencrantz and Guildenstern; *incoherence* of ideas and speech, so that his hearers are baffled or tantalized by unexpected associations of ideas; and *indecency* of speech, especially in company. These pretended symptoms are mostly words, although obviously the Prince can supplement them with obscene gestures or disrespectful postures (turning his back on the King, for instance). The antic disposition is that part of Hamlet's behavior and language which is assumed, according to tradition, for *concealment of his actual rationality.*

All of these symptoms, as Hamlet hopes, will be taken for those of actual madness, a madness which is the outgrowth of melancholia. There was no sharp line of difference between advanced melancholy and madness.[19] Now, note that Hamlet's deep melancholy produces signs which support the antic disposition though he does not deliberately assume them. Ophelia's description of his visit to her in her chamber (II.1.77-100) gives us many of them; negligence of his dress and person, unconscious discourtesy, pallor, and silence. Elsewhere we see him procrastinating, satirical, solitary, brooding painfully, even to the point of tears.

The present writer is one of those who believe that Hamlet,

despite two or three episodes of hysterical behavior, never is actually mad. If this is true, it follows that a careful student of the play can say with confidence that any given speech by the Prince is either a pretended piece of madness (the antic disposition) or is a rational speech, no matter how difficult it may be to evaluate the truth of the rational speech. To put the matter another way, notably in his soliloquies Hamlet's evaluation of his situation and his motives may not be true in the sense that he mistakenly magnifies, distorts, or overlooks some elements of his situation; but the connection of the thought and the relation to the events of the play are rational, though the mind of the speaker is somewhat diseased. It is really not very hard to distinguish Hamlet's assumed irrationality in the presence of others from his painful, perhaps mistaken, self-analysis.

In the ancient Norse story the Prince pretended madness to escape danger, for then the King could not accuse him of plotting even though everyone knew the Prince's motive for revenge. It has perplexed some critics that Shakespeare's Hamlet does not need to conceal his rationality by the antic disposition, for Claudius has no reason to fear Hamlet's revenge; Claudius believes himself the only person alive who knows about the murder. But the very ancientness of the pretended madness and its farcical humor doubtless made the audience think it essential to the story and so prevented Shakespeare from dropping the antic disposition. We can readily see that it lends grotesque humor at times; and we can concoct some other excuses for Shakespeare's retaining it, for instance, that if Claudius and Gertrude think Hamlet actually mad, they may betray their guilt by unguarded speeches in his presence.[20] But one might as well argue that Claudius should fear dangerous violence from an actual madman whose dislike for the King has been made apparent before.

At the end of Scene 5 the Prince feels an immense exhaustion of body and depression of spirit. But his courtesy remains, nevertheless; he apologizes for enforcing the oath of silence on good friends. As they stand back to let him precede, he insists on taking their arms, wearily, and all pass through the rear curtain and center door, by which they have entered.

Act II

SCENE 1. At the Globe Theater there was probably no intermission between Acts I and II. But with or without an intermission, we can see the purpose of Scene 1 readily enough—to inform the audience of the passage of about two months' time; enough time for Laertes to have arrived in Paris, run through his money, and sent home to Polonius for more. (The return of the emissaries sent to the King of Norway, in Scene 2, suggests this interval also.) However, this scene also returns to the ironic comedy which Polonius and his family contribute to the tragedy. The senility of the father is much more distinct here than in Act I; we see it in his prolixity, his repetition of phrases (*well said, very well said*), his use of several words to express the same idea (*such wanton, wild, and usual slips,/As are companions noted and most known*) and his forgetfulness (*What was I about to say? By the mass, I was about to say something. Where did I leave?*) Surely the weakness of an old man's mind ought to touch us as pathetic, not comic; but on the stage it usually has been comic.

To turn this enfeeblement of mind into comedy, Shakespeare allies it in Polonius with a strongly surviving self-conceit (64-68). Perhaps the worst aspect of old age is that it robs us of our concealments. The egoism that Polonius has been able in younger years to disguise by assumed modesty or humor or silence, he now prattles forth. And yet in commenting on his misjudgment of Hamlet's illness, he achieves a shrewd comment on old age (114-117).

In the commentary on I.5 we listed the additional causes of melancholy which the Ghost's revelation brought to Hamlet. These explain the amazing signs of melancholia Ophelia reports of him (75-100). Hamlet's clothing is dirty and disheveled,[21] he is pale and silent, he sighs profoundly, his look is anguished. So familiar are these symptoms of deep melancholy that the audience hardly needs Polonius's *Mad for thy love?* As Ophelia goes on to describe Hamlet's strange behavior, we can see why Shakespeare avoided dramatizing the scene: To show the hero in such an abject state would make him ridiculous—the pantomime could not be otherwise. But in narration this episode is suffused with Ophelia's pity. Her picture of Hamlet prepares us for his encounter with Polonius and Rosencrantz and Guildenstern.

SCENE 2. While Polonius is having his talk with Ophelia, in the castle's hall of state Claudius is welcoming two young visitors. The trumpets play a flourish and the King and Queen enter to take their places on thrones; then Rosencrantz and Guildenstern make their bows. These twin-like youths were Hamlet's companions before he went to University.[22] Having been so intimate with him, they should, thinks Claudius, be able to penetrate his melancholic isolation and find out what grievance (besides the pain of his father's death) is causing a mental state that is a menace to Claudius himself (7-10, 17). The young men's willingness to pry into Hamlet's heart to discover his deepest motives probably appeared more treacherous to the Elizabethans than it does to us, who are used to the practice of psychoanalysis. The Elizabethans often praised *faithful friendship.*

But even in 1600 it was well known that unless the cause of melancholia is discovered, treatment of the disease is bound to be unsuccessful.[23] Therefore, Shakespeare relies heavily on the reflection of Claudius's craft and treachery upon Rosencrantz and Guildenstern, in making the two men objects of satiric humor and contempt. After all, their primary (in fact, their only) motive is a zeal to please the King, in order thereby to benefit themselves. No doubt they are dressed in the height of fashion and a good deal alike. This equal foppishness would enhance the absurdity of their being indistinguishable in character, like interchangeable parts (33-34). Other than their fairly stupid self-interestedness, they are just about what Granville-Barker has called them, "One non-entity split into two." In addition to their plot-function, they serve as a foil to Hamlet and Claudius and for a mild satire on the courtier as a type.

The successful result of the embassage to Norway testifies to Claudius's skill in negotiation; it also prepares for a necessary event in Acts IV and V, the appearance of young Fortinbras upon the scene.

The Norwegian business being concluded, Polonius's complacency has free rein. He launches into a miniature classical oration which purports to discuss madness. Not all parts of a formal oration are here, but Kittredge has distinguished the exor-

A Commentary on the Action / Act II

dium (86-105), the narrative (106-146), and the peroration (147-151). Those in the audience who had had an education above the elementary ("dame school") level would recognize this travesty, and if they did not, Gertrude's plea, *More matter, with less art,* would stimulate them to perceive it. The burlesque oration increases the ludicrousness in Polonius's character, for whether he is conscious of using the forensic form, he is certainly pleased with his mastery of the arts of speech.

Part of his "narrative" is a letter of Hamlet's that Ophelia, on demand, has given up to Polonius, as she has also told him all about Hamlet's courting (126-128). Her contemptible subservience to her father has been commented on above, I.3. The letter itself sounds odd to our ears, of course not like the talk of Hamlet that we hear in the play, but rather, very formal and stilted.[24] Possibly its style was intended to suggest a young courtier's first love letter. At any rate, Hamlet himself admits its clumsiness and inexpressiveness near the end, and he closes with a more natural appeal that is winning.

In conclusion, Polonius names the successive stages of love-melancholy: despondency (*sadness*), rejection of food, wakefulness (*a watch*), physical weakness, hallucinations, and finally complete irrationality. (Of course we have not seen these exemplified in Hamlet or heard elsewhere that he has passed through them; and in fact he has not.) Claudius is not convinced that love is the cause of Hamlet's melancholy, though Gertrude, perhaps because of guilt about her own remarriage (56-57), is inclined to accept the diagnosis. So the device of spying on the lovers when alone is proposed by Polonius and accepted by Claudius. And now, ironically, the subject of their discussion comes unexpectedly on to the stage, pacing slowly, "seriously" absorbed in a book, as Gertrude remarks. The King and Queen hurry unceremoniously off stage at the opposite door, hustled by Polonius, who remains to *board* the Prince, as soldiers board an enemy ship at sea.

Note that this short interview (Hamlet's and Polonius's first one alone together) is not part of the spying scene just now planned. Then what purpose does it serve? Ophelia's description of Hamlet has prepared the audience for his greatly enhanced melancholy and his change in appearance. Indeed Shakespeare might have omitted this talk with Polonius and substituted the *To be or not to be* soliloquy that marks Hamlet's entry to the spying (or "Nunnery") Scene, III.1.56-89. But at that later point

Shakespeare may wish to dramatize Hamlet's violent oscillations between exultant anticipation and deep depression. Here there is no need for emphasizing dejection.

Perhaps the most that can be said about the present interview is that Polonius's vain confidence in his understanding of Hamlet's condition is ironically turned into bafflement by Hamlet's contemptuous wit. It is evident that Hamlet will not be easily victimized by the conceited old counsellor and his master. Hamlet's is still a very agile mind; he remains a dangerous antagonist.

Hamlet's saying that Polonius is a fishmonger has produced various interpretations. It is hard to believe that the slang sense of "bawd" could have failed to come to Shakespeare's mind and the audience's. If "bawd" is understood, it heightens both the humor of the image of *fish monger* (usually a coarse old woman) as applied to Polonius and the insult offered to him. Inevitably, one makes a connection of the sense "bawd" with Hamlet's warning about conception from walking in the sun (185-187). What precisely does *walk i' th' sun* mean? "Visit places of public amusement (and seduction)"—Kittredge's interpretation—is probably correct. To suppose that Hamlet is warning of Claudius's lustfulness (*sun* being the symbol of the king) is not clearly supported by any other passage in the play, and, of course, it is a meaning not suspected by Polonius. True, the point of this episode is that Polonius is stupid compared to Hamlet, and he might therefore fail to see the application. But in a verbal set-to in which the antic disposition allows Hamlet to be extravagant in speech, Shakespeare probably did not expect the audience to go beyond a proverbial sense for *walk i' th' sun*. The whole warning, then, might be paraphrased thus: "You obsequious old fool, in your stupidity don't allow your simpleton-daughter to go to theaters or masquerades—or you'll regret it.'

The insults are lost on Polonius, who only congratulates himself on having found the cause of madness, love for Ophelia. He annoys Hamlet with a further question, and in revenge Hamlet draws a satirical portrait of dotage, to be paralleled in many books. Though Polonius would like to brush it aside as the raving of a madman, it is so straightly pointed at himself that he is daunted, and, bowing rheumatically, he takes himself off. At the door he meets Rosencrantz and Guildenstern and must officiously point out the Prince, who is reading again.

In observing the first part of this reunion between the three

A Commentary on the Action / Act II

young men, we shall do well to think of the contrast between their costumes—Hamlet's black hose, doublet, and cloak,[25] disheveled and stained, and the gleaming satins, silver lace, and plumed hats of the two spies. This contrast heightens the dramatic effect of the characters' feeling. The pain and truth in Hamlet's dingy figure is set against the deceit and triviality of the gaudy-costumed friends. Despondent Hamlet, recognizing the faces of his old friends, offers his hand to each with delight and a warm greeting. But their fine clothing and deep bows enhance the artificiality of their speech, whose insincerity quickly chills Hamlet's pleasure at the reunion.

Their answers are self-conscious and evasive; to his question *What's the news?* (equivalent to "What are you doing here?") Rosencrantz answers meaninglessly, *The world's grown honest.* The word *honest* calls back all Hamlet's misery (*It is an honest ghost, that let me tell you,* I.5.138; *I would you were so honest a man,* line 176 of this scene). But pathetically hoping that some real friendliness survives in the youths, he tries to get a frank answer from them, without success. Their talk of *ambition* (258-266) reveals the thought running in their minds: "Is the Prince a dangerous malcontent because he has lost the throne he aspired to?" At last Hamlet extorts from them the admission that they did not come from love of him, but were sent for, to spy on him.

Profoundly miserable, he half defiantly tells the depth of his melancholy by describing how the world looks to a despairing mind (306-321). The passage is one of the most famous in all Shakespeare, a magnificent piece of poetic prose. It's latter half is a eulogy of man, which ends in sudden misanthropy. A great deal has been read into the whole speech; we may stop to glance at some of these interpretations.

The two halves of the speech are clearly parallel, for in the first half Hamlet tells how he responds to nature, the theater of man's exertions, and in the second what he thinks of man, the protagonist. In each half the first response is enthusiastic appreciation of beauty and power; but in each case this response is poisoned or corrupted into disgust. It is obvious that the first response of admiration is a universally felt one; the ensuing or accompanying disgust is perhaps more peculiar or temporary. Why does the disgust vanquish the admiration, in Hamlet's feeling? Perhaps in origin the pessimism is psychological, not philosophical, or in other words, it is the by-product of melancholia. The peculiar passions (fear and sorrow) of the melancholiac take such hold of his mind that his reason cannot overcome them and his view of the world is blackened by them. The shocking revelations of the last four months have produced a cynicism in Hamlet which makes him obsessed with the bestiality of man and which in turn may poison his very feeling about nature, also, though such an attitude is against reason, in most Renaissance philosophy.

Pretty much in those terms the Elizabethan idea of melancholy might be applied to the famous speech. But the interpretation of "melancholiac pessimism" is greatly limited by the fact that Hamlet is by no means a perfect clinical example of melancholy; for instance, he is not fearful, irritable,[26] lethargic, or subject to hallucinations. For this reason, and also because critics generally feel that the tragedy is to be explained on a higher level, they have searched lines and the play to extricate an underlying philosophy. What may strike any reader of the passage is that Hamlet does not mention God, any divinity, any abode of the supernatural, or life hereafter. (His reference to an *angel* and a *god* is merely as a poetical figure.) These are strange omissions by a studious man much given to reflection, who has even recently interviewed a supernatural visitor.

Inevitably, therefore, this and other episodes in which we might expect to find reference to God and religious ideas, but do not find them, lead to the supposition that Hamlet is an infidel or pagan thinker, possibly a Stoic who does not look for immortality, possibly a skeptic.[27] To see Hamlet as a skeptic, involved in a medieval story of barbaric motives and attitudes, results in making him a type of Renaissance man, or even modern man, as some believe—one whose religious faith and orthodox philosophy have been shattered by doubts due to new perspectives in science and philosophical concepts of man partly new, partly ancient. This seems to be the interpretation of Professor Battenhouse, who thinks the Apostrophe on Man in this scene expresses the misery of Renaissance skeptics cut off from Christian philosophy (especially the Scholastic) and wavering between incompatible views of man, man as angel, and man as beast. Having abandoned God, grace, and Revelation, the skeptic cannot fix man in his unique place in the scale of being, a creature who wonderfully combines an animal body with a spiritual soul, which should be governed by reason, and aided by grace. Instead, looked at one way, man seems almost preternatural in his mind and capacities; looked at another way, his reason leads him into corrup-

A Commentary on the Action / Act II

tion and disaster that even the irrational beasts avoid.[28] Hamlet's agonizing uncertainty is the predicament of skeptics since the Renaissance.

At this point Rosencrantz makes a neat transition by moving from the macrocosm (man in the universe) to the microcosm of the theater; he tells Hamlet of the coming of the actors. In 341-379 we have the most famous allusion to contemporary affairs in all Shakespeare. Historically, the background of the conversation is this: For about one hundred years dramatic performances by choir boys had become common in England. Cathedrals and chapels with sufficient income maintained choirs of boy sopranos; for the training of these groups to high perfection, they must live in a school and profit from daily instruction. Like other schoolboys, these lads had the usual subjects of study, including literature; and like other schoolboys, they acted plays in order to practice the language arts and train the memory. The choir-schoolboys were distinguished by superior voices, better articulation, and better rendering of songs. After a time some enterprising masters began to offer public performances of amusing plays. In the course of several generations a custom of professional production of plays became established. The profit was great enough to bring the boy companies (as they came to be called) into professional and economic competition with the adult acting companies of men, most of whom were resident in London theaters. Two companies in particular came into full activity (after a lapse of some years) in 1598, the Boys of St. Paul's Choir School and the Boys of the Chapel Royal in the Blackfriars district. As *Hamlet* was produced around 1600, we can see that Shakespeare is decidedly concerned about the successful competition from these children.[29]

The older generation of playwrights generally continued to write for the adult players. A number of young, new dramatists specialized in satiric comedies for the boy companies. The two groups began to satirize one another as personalities. So developed the "War of the Theaters," a term not very apt, for the contest was chiefly between Ben Jonson and one or two adversaries. Shakespeare's participation in it was small, but his company, the Lord Chamberlain's Men, was much affected by the new development in the world of the theater.

After the discussion of the "War" Hamlet's conversation with Rosencrantz and Guildenstern ends on an ironic note. He admits that his welcome of the players will appear more enthusiastic than his welcome of the seeming friends, and he tells, in antic fashion, the reason why: He is mad only when the wind is north-northwest;[30] at other times he knows a friend from a spy. The riddling speech is intended to mystify the faithless pair of courtiers. As Polonius comes on importantly to announce the arrival of the players, Hamlet continues his antic disposition by baffling him, refusing to listen to his news and singing scraps of a crude ballad at him.[31] This is an interlude of broad comedy in "the mad Hamlet" tradition; its entertainment of the audience seems its only purpose. But with the entrance of the players, a most congenial quality of Hamlet emerges, his enthusiasm for the theater.

Perhaps his burst of joy at their coming is another symptom of his melancholy, an abnormal swing of his emotion from deep depression to irrational happiness. Quite often Hamlet clearly does react from one extreme of feeling to the other. Perhaps his enthusiasm for the players is a subconscious mechanism of escape from what appears to him an insoluble problem of vengeance. It may in fact be both of these, but also it is true that his love of the theater dates from before his father's death and may properly be accepted as an element of his normal temperament, and an appealing one.

His taste in dramatic style has been criticized by those who find the Pyrrhus speech bombastic and absurd. But "bombastic" is perhaps not the exact word to describe the style. The narrative passage is old-fashioned, somewhat too heavily rhetorical and figurative. The rhythm is strong and insistent, though not monotonous; the verbal music of vowels and consonants is sonorous. No doubt Shakespeare wanted a passage of heroic verse that would deal with a familiar, classical theme of brutal vengeance. Pyrrhus's vengeance for Achilles' death would serve as a kind of foil to Hamlet's revenge, still kept from actuality by Hamlet's sick mind. Pyrrhus, the elemental killer, and Hamlet, the melancholiac, are directly opposed. And the fall of Troy was a theme of legendary greatness to Englishmen, who were the offspring of Brut, great grandson of Aeneas. So Shakespeare decided that an heroic style, but one slightly archaic, would be the mode for this recitation. The tone of the Pyrrhus passage reminds us of Senecan drama; but it does not burlesque it. It contrasts with the fluent colloquialism in which *Hamlet* is written. There is a strong thematic connection with the soliloquy which soon follows; but there is also a sharp stylistic contrast that makes the soliloquy all the more effective (*For Hecuba!—What's Hecuba to him?*).

A Commentary on the Action / Act II

Hamlet's swearing and rudeness to Polonius are unabated, but his satiric instructions to the old man about the players have a tone that is almost sober, as a preparation for the soliloquy. His proposal to the First Player to insert a dozen or more lines in "The Murder of Gonzago" need not worry us, for no one has been able to detect which lines they are, if in fact Claudius does not put an end to "Gonzago" before they are spoken.

The second of Hamlet's major soliloquies ends this scene. It consists substantially of two themes. One is a "self-castigation" (characteristic of melancholy),[32] on the one hand, for his own apathy, and on the other, for his failure to kill Claudius. The second theme is his justification for using the play-within-the-play to prove Claudius's guilt. We may briefly examine the development of these two themes.

The self-reproach for his own lack of emotion is very natural, though not logical. Melancholy men were thought to be lethargic, half paralyzed, as it were, by their passions of fear and grief. Hamlet's grief for his father's *damn'd defeat* and for his mother's crimes has produced in him long sessions of agonized meditation which he now considers to be shameful inaction or lethargy, and emotionally, as a sort of numbness or despairing apathy. The First Player's simulated grief as he recites the death of Priam renews Hamlet's consciousness of his own dull, dead grief. He feels guilty that he has not shown the world a greater passion than the Player's. The mistake here is, of course, Hamlet's forgetting that such a display would have put him in peril of confinement as a madman; and furthermore, the mere display of passion usually accomplishes little in life (Hamlet, in fact, seems to confuse life and the stage—*He would drown the stage with tears,* etc.).

Hamlet then passes from this fallacious self-reproach to one more convincing—that he has *done* nothing about revenge. The underlying assumption here seems to be that the killing of Claudius must be immediately actuated by passion; but this idea also is a fallacy. A determination to kill based on intellectual conviction would serve much better. But Hamlet's mental illness is such that he feels that if only he had the proper fury against Claudius, the killing would be easy. Therefore he tries to lash himself into the fury—but to what good? His intended victim is not present, and the momentary, hysterical outburst which Hamlet achieves (608-610) at once seems even to himself a futile, silly business.

In disgust and exhaustion he turns back to the idea that has already occurred to him (562-569), the play of "The Mouse-

Trap," as he later calls it. He (as does Shakespeare) relies on the ancient tradition that a criminal will break down and publicly confess his crime if he witnesses a re-enactment of it on the stage. If Claudius so much as winces (626-627), that will be proof enough for Hamlet. But critics have often questioned, "Is not this mere procrastination? Hamlet has stated his faith in the Ghost's word. What more proof does he need?"

However, Hamlet's own defense (627-633) has enough theological truth to answer these questions. As the Prince says, the spirit that he has seen may be the devil, who, on the authority of many learned men of that age, found the disease of melancholy a source of weakness in men by which to tempt them into crime and damnation. Shakespeare perhaps shared this common belief; certainly he is utilizing it here. Indeed, the devil, it was believed, would speak truth if by so doing he could delude a soul into evil. Both Horatio and Hamlet have used the devices of religious adjuration and close observation of the Ghost to determine whether it is a good or diabolical spirit; and Hamlet, at least, is at first emotionally convinced it is his father's spirit. But he is right in concluding that he must find a further, wholly rational test of the Ghost's truth, for a first judgment could too easily be wrong, and the results would be eternally disastrous for Hamlet if he were misled by a demon.

Claudius's response to "The Murder of Gonzago," which Hamlet calls "The Mouse-Trap," is acceptable to the Elizabethan audience as a valid test of the King's guilt, and therefore of the Ghost's truth. Especially will this be so if Horatio's observation of Claudius agrees with Hamlet's (III.2.89-92, 297-299). The only question that remains is why Hamlet has not applied this or some other test earlier, why he has let two months pass since his meeting with the Ghost without doing anything. To answer that no other safe test has occurred to him is not satisfactory, for we should expect a man of his intelligence to think of the play-test and send for the actors. But, quite obviously, the lethargy and overcarefulness which are characteristic of deep melancholy have prevented him from acting with initiative and ingenuity. The shocks suffered from the Ghost's revelation have sunk Hamlet too far into melancholy. The arrival of the players is just a lucky accident that he is able to utilize.

Dramatically, the play-within-the-play is thoroughly valid. It offers a bit of unusual *spectacle* on stage, and fine dramatic *irony;* but above all it offers *suspense.*

Act III

SCENE 1. If this play, which is long even in the cut Folio version, was broken by two intermissions, it is possible that the first one came at the end of Act II.

When the music between the acts has fallen silent, the trumpets have sounded a flourish, and the action has resumed, very little time has elapsed at Elsinore (II.2.565, III.1.21). It is the following morning, and Claudius has summoned Rosencrantz and Guildenstern to report what they have learned about Hamlet's cause of melancholy. But they have disappointingly little to tell, nothing, in fact, until Gertrude's loving concern for Hamlet prompts her to ask if they have tried recreation with him. Then they remember the play to be given, and Claudius seems glad that Hamlet can think of anything else besides his mysterious grievance. "Most happily" will the King attend "The Mouse-Trap," though while he speaks, he is planning a mouse-trap for Hamlet, with Ophelia as bait. When Rosencrantz and Guildenstern have been dismissed, Claudius explains the plan to Gertrude, whose kindly feeling toward Ophelia is a notable aspect of her character (38-42).

Walk you here, says Polonius to Ophelia, directing her to walk back and forth within the inner stage, or before the center rear door, as she reads her prayerbook. This semblance of religion to cover up a worldly purpose bothers Polonius's conscience a little, perhaps because of his cruel separation of the lovers two months before. But his moralizing comment (46-49) may be not so much a self-accusation as a device to introduce Claudius's remorseful soliloquy.

The soliloquy needs a little preparation because it is a surprising revelation. Thus far the King has seemed completely self-possessed, resourceful, and determined. From his smooth exterior we should not have guessed what he now reveals, sharp pangs of guilt.[33] They do not diminish his power as an antagonist to Hamlet, but they show him much more human and deepen the tragedy in another dimension. It is also interesting to observe that Shakespeare here prepares the audience for "The Mouse-Trap" scene by establishing the King's guilt, thus allowing them to observe more appreciatively the signs of his breakdown during the play-within-the-play, as well as to listen more closely to Hamlet. Of course, some dramatic irony is lost, but greater ease of comprehension of a rather complex scene is achieved. In addition, the present soliloquy also prepares for Claudius's complete self-revelation in the "Prayer Scene" after "The Mouse-Trap."

The King and Polonius now exit, but reappear in the upper stage peeping from behind curtains or else at one of the upper windows overlooking the stage. They probably become visible there about the time Hamlet finishes his soliloquy.

Entering from a side door opposite to the King's and Polonius's exit, Hamlet does not observe Ophelia, half-hidden by the curtain. He moves downstage, perhaps to lean against one of the pillars supporting the "Heavens" as he begins his meditation.

His most famous speech, *To be or not to be,* comes only fifty-five lines after his second soliloquy, and even if we allow for the additional psychological distance of a ten-minute intermission for the audience, we should be surprised if in the present soliloquy Shakespeare offered us any new facet of character or great revulsion of feeling in Hamlet. In fact he does not. It has been suggested that about fifteen hours of waiting for the critical test of "The Mouse-Trap" has had the effect of plunging Hamlet down from the exhilaration generated by the arrival of the players into the profound hopelessness expressed in this soliloquy. But our comments on the meditation at the end of II.2 stressed its elements of very characteristic melancholy. Obviously, the *To be or not to be* soliloquy expresses as a primary element the morbid wish for death that was uppermost in the First Soliloquy and that is also a familiar symptom of melancholia.

But note that the wish for death is stated in terms of a philosophic problem for all men, not as the Prince's own highly personal yearning. Hamlet does not mention any peculiar circumstances of his own situation or temperament. Human life viewed in a general way raises the question, Why should not most men commit suicide? Both the question and the answer that Hamlet proposes are philosophical propositions. As such, the most notable thing about them is their exclusion of any direct reference to Deity, grace, a personal judgment, and heaven or hell. With regard to an afterlife and anything it may imply about the realities just listed, Hamlet speaks of it as a mysterious possibility; that is all

A Commentary on the Action / Act III

it appears to him to be. As in the "Apostrophe on Man" Hamlet here seems to be a skeptic.[34]

Some of the terms of the speech have, of course, been used in Christian thought and can be given a forced Christian implication—for instance, *sleep* (64) as "soul-sleep," and *conscience* (83), which, however, is used here in the sense of "reflection" or "conscious *thought*." Significant is Hamlet's blaming *thought* (85) for mankind's cowardice about suicide. *Thought* is a common Elizabethan term for melancholy; by its implication of "fear," meaning fear of the unknown, Hamlet's own disease becomes figuratively the affliction of all mankind.

You will do well to look up the Elizabethan sense of key terms in this soliloquy, such as *rub, coil, respect, time, patient, quietus, puzzles.*

Ophelia, who has stood still, perhaps, during most of this soliloquy, now enters the outer stage, timidly continuing her pretense of reading her devotions. Hamlet turns and sees her, her prayer-book, and her nervous manner. He perceives that the meeting has been pre-arranged, and probably not by her initiative. He addresses her as *nymph* and asks that she remember him in her prayers, a request that sounds like devoted respect. But unfortunately *nymph* was then a word of many associations, one of which is suggested by Dekker's phrase *nymphs of Picthatch* (a suburb in which were many brothels). Ophelia does not answer Hamlet's greeting with phrases such as we might expect, "My lord, I do pray for you. Please pray for me." Her response seems to evade recognition of his insulting ambiguity; she says in effect, "My lord, we have not met for a long time." If Hamlet's greeting still seems too unkind or insulting to be possible here, note that all his replies to her are either strange or very rude. In short, Hamlet seems to put on his antic disposition when he *first* observes Ophelia, not later, at 103.

She returns his gifts with a reproach for his being *unkind*. As she has refused to see him and has returned his letters, in obedience to her father, this reproach is mystifying; she herself has been the unkind one. Perhaps an adequate explanation is the rudeness which he is displaying at this moment. His entrance into her chambers (II.1.77-100), staring silently, with his clothing all loosened, seems to us a sign of a pitiable distraction; but to Ophelia it was conduct not different from the rudeness with which he has treated her when they have met publicly since then, when he has been acting his madness. We should prefer to have her pity him for his affliction. But she apparently is hurt by his rudeness, or else she is obeying Polonius's command to treat Hamlet severely, in order to test his devotion.

Hamlet's response to her severity is crushing to her, and confounding to Polonius. Hamlet harshly demands, "Are you chaste (*honest*)?" and then gives her a cruel lecture on the treachery of men and the need to save her own virtue by getting to a nunnery. Hamlet acts as madly as possible. Midway, perhaps at line 132, it may occur to Hamlet that Polonius and Claudius are listening, and he grows more violent. His denunciation of men, women, and marriage is another symptom of melancholy, that is, bitter misanthropy. If Polonius has hoped to see Hamlet kneel and plead for Ophelia's love and favor, Hamlet has most thoroughly frustrated him. The only conclusion that the two eavesdroppers can draw is that Hamlet is melancholy-mad, which is what they knew before. There seems no likelihood that friendlier relations with Ophelia will cure him.

While the two observers are descending backstage, Ophelia speaks her eulogy of the former Hamlet and lament for the ruin of their loves. Though there is good reason to think that Hamlet was formerly all that she says he was, the style in which she expresses her lament has an artificiality of rhetorical form, of figures of speech, and of devices of sound that deprives her of some of the sympathy one might expect her situation to bring her. Shakespeare seems to guard against allowing Ophelia to share as largely in the drama as Juliet does, for instance, by not giving Ophelia speeches of natural passion.

When Claudius and Polonius enter, the King's decisiveness is again evident, as in I.2. He senses that Hamlet's passions are not effects of love, and that Hamlet, though melancholy, is not really mad. Both the melancholy and the passions, therefore, are probably directed against himself. Hypocritically, he asks Polonius whether a change of scene, a visit to England, will not be curative for Hamlet? Polonius is obstinate. While approving the proposed cure, he insists that *neglected love* must really be the cause, and asks permission to try another eavesdropping trick; for Polonius's ways of discovering people's motives are all one kind—spying. (See his advice to Reynaldo, II.1). Though it will be Gertrude's love that extricates Hamlet's secret griefs, it will be Polonius who will recognize them. But the audience knows that his senile persistence will be fatal to him.

A Commentary on the Action / Act III 41

SCENE 2. At last night has come, supper is over, and Hamlet has summoned the players to make sure that the *dozen or sixteen lines* he provided yesterday have been inserted in "The Murder of Gonzago" and will be spoken effectively. He has even read the passage to them as he would like it to be spoken (1-2). But having done what most people would consider enough to clarify his wishes, Hamlet cannot resist giving this captive audience of experts his own views on the art of acting, certainly a subject of consuming interest to him. He does not seem to be the melancholy Hamlet, or even the tragic Hamlet. In fact, he is probably facetious Master Shakespeare speaking through Hamlet's mouth and cracking a joke at his good friends and fellow-actors by lecturing them. This interpretation is supported by the ironic brevity of the First Player's answers, which may be paraphrased as "You're absolutely right, sir," "We've taken care of that little item, sir." Meanwhile, his mates wink and grin at one another as the royal amateur instructs them in their business.

In general, Hamlet's criticisms show very good sense and taste; they also imply a high standard of technique among Elizabethan actors, for otherwise his witty observations would be futile. To discuss the implications of his criticisms in detail is unnecessary here. It is enough to caution the student against thinking Hamlet means he wants a very naturalistic, restrained style of acting. Though he objects to ranting and extravagant posturing, his remarks still leave unshaken the traditional view that Elizabethan acting was in general more declamatory and more stylized than our own. Recall the *To be or not to be* soliloquy: In actual life such a meditation would be spoken (if spoken at all) in a dry monotone, the melancholiac being almost motionless, perhaps with his head bent. This manner would not do even in a modern arena theater. We can be sure that Richard Burbage found means to vitalize the speech with action and charge its phrases with significance as they rang through the Globe Theater.

As the players go out to dress (*make ready,* 49-50), Hamlet calls in Horatio. The Prince's friend and confidant has been absent from the play through all of Act II, but now we learn that he probably never went back to Wittenberg after the Ghost's visit, about two months ago. Or if he went back to the university, he has again returned to Elsinore and been with Hamlet recently (81-82). There is a looseness in structure of plot here, for Horatio's dropping out of sight in Act II has heightened Hamlet's isolation in his deepest melancholy and need of a friend; yet the disappearance remains unexplained. But note that the substance of Act II has been only the events of *one day*. Though in large measure a revelation of the paralyzing mental state to which Hamlet has fallen in the course of two months, its various incidents have not obviously demanded the presence of Horatio. In short, when the play is on stage, the audience are not conscious of Horatio's incongruous disappearance.

Hamlet has dismissed Polonius, Rosencrantz, and Guildenstern with contemptuous rudeness. Therefore, his compliment to Horatio (59-60) is the more surprising and pleasing: "You are as complete a man as ever I met." Horatio tries to brush the compliment aside, bowing gravely to relieve his embarrassment. But Hamlet insists that he has no motive for merely flattering a poor gentleman, one as out of power as Hamlet himself. Then in fluent blank verse he outlines beautifully the strength of the Stoic character as he believes Horatio shows it and as he would like to have it (70-79). That strength is impassivity, the self-command that despises fortune, good and bad. The play gives us no striking dramatization of this virtue in Horatio, but we see him in action enough to believe Hamlet's description is true. However, no doubt the function of Horatio as foil, or contrast, to Hamlet is as much based on this passage as on any episode of the play.

Thus the eulogy comments obliquely on Hamlet's own character, and suggests the nobility of his mind which, though sick with melancholy, is able to praise one which is superior to passion. But the expression of love which underlies the praise is also a needed preparation for Hamlet's disclosure that he has confided in Horatio about the Ghost's message. We are much less surprised to hear this news after feeling the warmth of friendship implied in the compliment. Thus Shakespeare expertly weaves together the different elements of his pattern.

And now at last it is time for the play that Hamlet thinks will release him from doubt and make action possible. The kettledrums roll a Danish march, the trumpets sound the flourish, and the royal party take their places. Probably the thrones for Claudius and Gertrude are in front of the curtain that covers the inner stage opening; Polonius and Ophelia and one or two others are seated on chairs at Claudius's right; the other male attendants sit on the floor or stand; and the whole party face downstage toward the audience. Hamlet, of course, seats himself on the floor with his head at Ophelia's knees, a position conventional at Court perform-

A Commentary on the Action / Act III

ances. He is able to turn and watch Claudius very easily. The greater part of the outer stage and one or two doors at the left are available for the use of the players.

After Hamlet's bitter, indecent jibes at his guests (thus he plays his antic disposition), the actors silently enter and present a dumb-show. A dumb-show is a pantomime of one episode or several episodes of a dramatic story, enacted in simplified form. It may serve any of a number of dramatic purposes; probably most commonly. it is an exposition of part of the story that must be known, but is not felt to be so significant as other parts. The purpose of the dumb-show in *Hamlet* is clearly twofold. (1) It summarizes Act I of "The Murder of Gonzago"; but this function surely would be unnecessary if "The Murder" were presented independently, outside of *Hamlet*. (2) But because the audience in the Globe Theater is supposed to concentrate on Claudius's response to "The Murder," it cannot at the same time watch closely a second play being acted in front of the King. Therefore, Shakespeare provides the Globe patrons with the theme and a summary of the first act of "The Murder," after which they will be free to give only slight attention to Gonzago and Baptista, concentrating rather on Claudius.

Not uncommonly plays began with a dumb-show;[35] hence Claudius sees nothing suspicious in the device. And though he is shocked to see his crime re-enacted, the action of the dumb-show is so rapid that the thing is over very quickly, and he is able to keep his composure. Alarmed as he is, he must immediately decide what to do—whether to leave the hall, thus betraying his distress, or to try to face it out. By experience he knows that dumb-shows are often only *preliminary* exposition, not summaries of what is to follow. He therefore says nothing. A Prologue appears, and after waiting politely for the unruly Prince to be quiet, speaks a stanza which tells Claudius—nothing at all. The King sits stolidly as Hamlet glares at him, Horatio stares at him, and the Player King and Queen begin their interminable discussion of their love. "The Murder" is written in rhymed couplets and in a sententious, old-fashioned style, to contrast with the more natural style of *Hamlet*. "The Murder" tortures Claudius by its slow pace and its insistence on ideas and feelings that wring his conscience. Worst of all, and at last unendurable, are Hamlet's biting comments, which reveal to Claudius that the Prince, somehow, has learned about the murder.[36] When Lucianus has poured the poison in Gonzago's ears and Hamlet's taunting voice interrupts again, Claudius can endure no more, turns his contorted face aside, rises, calls for a torch-bearer, and hurries away.

The Globe audience is thrilled by the success of Hamlet's device, and he himself is excited almost to hysterical delight, singing a ballad and perhaps dancing a few steps. So wrought up is he that, though still in the guise of madness, he tells the spies Rosencrantz and Guildenstern enough about the real cause of his melancholy to endanger his life; he admits his "ambition" (354). This will be great news for the pair to report to Claudius. Now the contest between the King and Hamlet will employ all the craft each can muster, and no quarter given. Hamlet's triumph has put him in grave peril. But he rides the crest of his mood of triumph a few moments more, flaying Guildenstern and befooling Polonius. In fact, this exultation probably gives him the false confidence that now, if chance gave the opportunity, he could kill the King. Since the King is safely withdrawn out of reach, Hamlet will, instead, bring his mother to confession and repentance of her guilt by scourging her with words. The short soliloquy is careful preparation for dramatic ironies soon to follow.

SCENE 3. This, the famous "Prayer Scene," opens with Claudius's first move against Hamlet, the prompt decision to send him to England. Probably Rosencrantz and Guildenstern, his escorts, suspect this mission is for Hamlet's exile or death. But they accept the commission. As Hamlet later says, *They make love to the employment* (V.2.57), without realizing its danger.

When the chairs were removed from the stage after the play-within-the-play (while Hamlet sang his ballad), one was left near the rear door. Now that he is alone, Claudius sits down meditating agonizingly upon his guilt, which he has just taken steps to augment and confirm by the death of Hamlet. (To be sure, he is now fighting for his own life.) "The Murder of Gonzago" now attains its full effect; horror and fear of hell overwhelm him. Even more impressive than his remorse is his honest and clear appraisal of his soul-state. He knows he lacks true repentance, which must include renunciation of the worldly satisfactions—sovereign power and the possession of Gertrude—which led him to defy the will of God. Forgiveness will not come as long as his "repentance" is only a fear that leads to no submission. And yet he yearns to be at peace with Heaven and to be able to pray. He rises, turns, and kneels against the chair, to *make assay.*

Hamlet, entering from the side to cross the stage, is startled

A Commentary on the Action / Act III 45

to see how quickly Opportunity has favored him. The scene has manifold ironies. Deceived, probably, by his own fluctuation of emotion, Hamlet has thought himself ready to drink hot blood (III.2.408), unhesitatingly to drive the dagger into his enemy; and so Fate obligingly gives the perfect opening. But the revenger finds that, after all, he is not ready to kill. And Claudius, who has just begun to arrange Hamlet's death, unconsciously drops his guard and invites attack.

The real reasons why Hamlet does not stab his enemy have been much discussed. The reason which the prince himself offers was a traditional one in stories of revenge: In essence it is that revenge is only partial unless it includes eternal damnation. The enemy must be inveigled into some sinful act—blasphemy, lechery, drunkenness—and slain in the instant of the sin, without time for repentance. Such a motive is so far beyond Christian charity that even when revenge tragedy was most popular, only horrible villains would act upon it. Most critics, therefore, have decided that it is not Hamlet's real motive at all, merely one trumped up to rationalize his inability to strike. (Some, however, accept the reason as true, and conclude that Hamlet has given way to virulent hatred.) An extreme alternative to Hamlet's stated reason is the argument that subconsciously he does not want to commit murder, that his conscience will *never* allow him to kill Claudius by premeditated act. A second alternative is that Hamlet is too civilized and honorable to strike a defenseless man. "The speech is merely a pretext for delay," says Kittredge, i.e., until Claudius can be confronted with his rapier drawn. You way weigh these and other alternatives and make your own decision, hinging it on your general interpretation of Hamlet's character.

In any event, Claudius is not a repentant sinner, as Hamlet seems to think, and so the Prince's long rationalization is irrelevant—another irony.

SCENE 6. This, the "Closet Scene," is even more ironical than the preceding, for Hamlet's misunderstanding of his situation is more evident. He has failed to kill the King because Chance surprised him with the proffer before he was ready (?). But the punishment of his mother is his own plan, and it is to be verbal; and whatever else may be thought of him, no one has denied Hamlet a supreme facility with words. Yet his exhortation of his mother has no visible effect.

The excitement of the play-within-a-play is still on him, and the sight of Claudius at his mercy has not diminished it. When he enters, his manner is so violent that Gertrude is frightened and tries to leave. Polonius cries out, is stabbed—and Gertrude is convinced that Hamlet is a dangerous maniac. Trembling, she sits and listens while her wild-eyed son launches into a fierce denunciation of her sin—but what is it? Hamlet cannot bring himself to say *adultery*, for she believes that none but Claudius and herself know of it, and how should Hamlet have learned of it? She appears innocent of any knowledge of the killing of King Hamlet (30). At last he realizes he has to denounce her for the marriage only, a marriage based solely on shameful *lust* (he does not mention *incest*, though it may be understood between them). His idea of sex in middle-life appears positively naïve, though we should allow for the present frustration which may make him less intelligent than usual. Probably this sense of frustration causes him to rise into a shouting fury against Claudius just before the Ghost appears.

The Ghost enters in a costume appropriate for this room, probably in a dressing gown (135). Gertrude has been seated in the same chair against which Claudius kneeled; it is turned a little toward the center where Polonius lies, so that the Ghost's entrance from the same door as in Act 1 is behind her. Hamlet, facing her, suddenly breaks off in the midst of his tirade, looks past her, and speaks with awe to—nothingness, she thinks (105). As the ability of a spirit to make itself visible only to chosen persons was an accepted fact of the supernatural, Gertrude's inability to see the Ghost is not evidence that Hamlet has an hallucination. On the contrary, hallucinations were not generally made visible to the audience in the Elizabethan theater (for instance, the dagger that leads Macbeth to sleeping Duncan). Hamlet's Ghost is visible and real.

It is less easy to be sure why Shakespeare uses the Ghost again at this point. If we measure story-time carefully, we may feel that Hamlet has not really delayed the revenge beyond reason, except for one forfeited opportunity. But if we consider the events that have occupied Acts II and III, we may indeed feel that much entertainment and excitement have occurred, but that Hamlet has not progressed at all toward his objective, and that this seeming delay has been capped by his failure in the Prayer Scene. Worse than this, the killing of Polonius has doomed the mad Prince to death in exile. But if the intervention of the Ghost is intended to renew the urgency of Hamlet's duty, the immediate effects are not easy to point to. Hamlet goes on with his lecture to his mother in a slightly lower key, but in imagery nearly as disgusting and at great length. In Act IV he appears much the same Hamlet as before, alternately in his antic disposition or his melancholic self-reproach. Possibly the return of the Ghost in this scene is an episode of the old *Hamlet* play that Shakespeare retained without full justification.

Like Hamlet's sex-nausea, his hatred of Claudius is more evident in this scene than anywhere else. If *Taint not thy mind* (I.5.85) means "Do not give away to hate," Hamlet has sinned. For this reason lines 172-175 have seemed to some critics a key passage in the tragedy. These critics believe that, since the command to avenge was delivered by Divine will, Hamlet must execute it like a Divine agent, in a spirit of justice, without malice toward Claudius. This spirit he certainly has violated in the Prayer Scene and in this one. In addition, the killing of Polonius is hard to justify on grounds of self-defense. Though Hamlet's enemy, the King, is a very cunning villain now roused to awareness of his own danger, capable of any treachery, and in command of many agents to do his will, on the other hand, Claudius, whom Hamlet has just seen at prayer, would hardly choose to have Hamlet assassinated in his mother's presence. Hamlet must be considered guilty of an impulsive killing, or manslaughter, due in some part to his passionate resentment against his mother. Therefore, Hamlet, who is Heaven's scourge of evil-doers (including Polonius, who conspired against Hamlet's election), has himself become a guilty man who must learn repentance or suffer punishment—or both.

For those who take the Ghost as an evil force inciting Hamlet to evil, the line *I must be their scourge and minister* shows Hamlet "encroaching on the role of providence . . . play[ing] at God."[37] Various causes have been assigned for this egoism or neurosis (or whatever it may be) that leads the hero astray. The degree of his guilt is stated variously, depending on the critic's diagnosis of the fault in Hamlet's character.

Act IV

SCENE 1. Gertrude tells Claudius of the killing of Polonius, a piece of news less surprising, but more dreadful, than she has feared it will be. She does not seem to have supposed that Hamlet was striking at Claudius when he stabbed through the arras; but Claudius knows that. He has escaped death. On the other hand, the killing of the chief councilor is dangerous to Claudius's new sovereignty, for it will provoke sharp criticism of his handling of the mad prince. Yet the Prince is too popular to be punished severely (IV.3.3-7).

Gertrude still tries to protect her son. She says nothing of Hamlet's savage abuse of Claudius to her, and she lies venially by saying Hamlet wept after the killing. Of course, she believes him to be dangerously mad, so that her love cannot justify her protesting against the exile to England. The play does not give any warrant for thinking Hamlet's tirade against her marriage makes any difference in her relations with Claudius.

SCENE 2. This is another episode of the traditional "mad Hamlet," the assumed antic disposition of insulting talk and crazy action.

SCENE 3. Claudius's speech (1-11) is in effect a soliloquy,[38] and thus gives due emphasis to his reason for using an indirect way of executing Hamlet. It is also preparatory for the bursting of the mob into the palace in Scene 5, following.

In this first confrontation of the two antagonists since the Play Scene, we feel, perhaps, some disappointment that the underlying feelings of the men cannot be revealed more openly and intensely. But each must play a part: Claudius must conceal his hatred and fear under the role of a grieving and unwilling judge; Hamlet may not drop the antic disposition, for without it he would at once be subject to trial and execution for treason. So we have to read their true feelings and purposes in the ambiguities of a few lines (48-49).

The King's final soliloquy (60-70) tells more of necessary cir-

A Commentary on the Action / Act IV

cumstances than of Claudius's inner state. Shakespeare reminds the audience that at this time England is subject to Denmark's king. The letters sent are closed ones, their contents unknown to the bearers. If Claudius has any scruples about this way of disposing of his enemy, they are submerged by the tide of his fear, and they are not uttered.

SCENE 4. The second, and longer, intermission in the Globe production of *Hamlet* perhaps was made between Scenes 3 and 4, or possibly after Scene 4. Since Scene 4 no doubt should be introduced by the thunder of drums, and certainly begins with the spectacle of an army marching across the stage, these attention-catchers may well mark the resumption of the play after intermission.

Fortinbras is to have a fairly important role in the denouement; therefore, it is good technique to introduce him in person, at least briefly, about midway in the play. More important than this fact is the dramatic usefulness of the parallel between Fortinbras and Hamlet, and especially the contrast of temperament. Even more than Horatio and Laertes, Fortinbras is a foil to Hamlet, a contrast to heighten our realization of Hamlet's qualities. And we are made to see the contrast through Hamlet's reaction to this rival. Fortinbras has not much to say here, but his words are characteristically incisive and simple.

His army enters with drum and colors, halts while he gives his dispatch to the Captain, then marches slowly off. (The Captain must, of course, go to Elsinore with the message and then overtake the army.) Hamlet and his friends enter as the rear of the company leave the stage, and Hamlet questions the Captain about the purpose of the expedition. The Prince's first response to the information seems to be wondering contempt for the absurdity of international conflicts—for the trifle that is being fought over, the absurdity of the forces, and the impossibility of settlement.[39]

But in the fourth (and last) major soliloquy of the play (32-66), we see that the attitude of contempt was only a pretense, a concealment of Hamlet's true feelings. As is true of most people, when a feeling of guilt and shame possesses him, his pride demands that he hide his feeling from others by affecting superiority. When alone, however, he admits to himself, *How all occasions* [events] *do inform against* [denounce] *me!* (*to myself* is understood). The chance meeting with the do-or-die adventurers shocks Hamlet into realizing the contrast between the daring that a normal man ought to use to accomplish his purposes and the painful scrupulosity about motives and futile weighing of chances of success which he has been involved in during the last two months. (So his own behavior looks to Hamlet; whether he sees it correctly is another matter.) The accidental meeting with Fortinbras denounces Hamlet to his own intelligence, convicting him of folly. Hence, the daring that is proper to man in an uncertain world, contrasted to Hamlet's over careful calculation of chances of success, is the principal theme of the soliloquy.

But there are minor themes. Hamlet wonders momentarily whether *bestial oblivion*, "forgetfulness like that of an animal" content to *sleep and feed,* may not have been the cause of his inaction. He also realizes more clearly the importance of honor, that is, men's esteem or respect, in his world. This, indeed, is the idea he has pretended to explode, in his remarks to the Captain. But he dwells on it in the climactic part of his soliloquy, and in fact he seems to substitute the idea of honor for any Divine command to be understood in the Ghost's message. Probably Shakespeare here is indicating a movement of Hamlet's mind toward the "serenity" or "acquiescence" (whatever the word should be) that everyone observes in Hamlet after his return to Denmark. The soliloquy also somewhat resembles the second major one (II.2.-576-634) in that it is a self-castigation for melancholy apathy. But this one is less forced in tone and is provoked by an episode of real human action, not by a fiction of art. The fact that Hamlet does not mention the Ghost's command does not indicate that the Prince rejects it; but his reviewing of his situation in terms of ordinary human motives, as if his mind were striving to deal with life's problems within the limitations that give men some hope of managing their affairs successfully—this may be significant of a degree of recovery from melancholy.

If this impression is true, it is not really impaired by Hamlet's statement that he has delayed revenge needlessly. The lines *Sith I have cause and will and strength and means/To do't* are hard to accept, in fact, seem contradictory of Hamlet's own earlier view of his predicament. Cause and will (as much as a melancholiac can muster), he certainly has had; but strength and means, if they mean moral confidence and circumstances in which he could kill Claudius, yet save his own life in order to justify his deed to Denmark—these he probably has *not* had. His intelligence here is clouded by his feeling of self-reproach.

A Commentary on the Action / Act IV

SCENE 5. A few days have elapsed. Hamlet has gone, to be absent during three scenes, 510 lines, about the normal length of an act. But he has left a crop of evils for Claudius to struggle with, and the audience finds no dullness in Scenes 5, 6, and 7. The pathos of Ophelia's madness is the first of several dramatic interests, and the dangerous result of the madness, the fury of Laertes, is the second and greater evil that Claudius must overcome.

We have had no forewarning of Ophelia's madness; Shakespeare uses surprise. But the play makes clear that the primary source of her madness is shock and grief over her father's death (see 4, 45, 76-77, 159-160). We have no reason to question Claudius's and Laertes's statements about the cause. True, some of Ophelia's symptoms resemble those of love-melancholy, which like other forms of melancholy is a source of madness; grief for the loss of Hamlet's love must have contributed to her distraction. But until the death of Polonius no change in her personality has been evident after her repelling of Hamlet two months ago. Furthermore, her repeated babbling about seduction is probably just another form of the indecent talk that was conventionally spoken by mad folk on the Elizabethan stage. Of course Hamlet's responsibility for her state is not less because he provoked it by killing her father, rather than by abandoning her.

Laertes's whole effort to avenge the dishonor done to his father and himself offers a parallel to Hamlet's delayed revenge, and the characters of the two young men are necessarily contrasted. Laertes is driven to lead an insurrection by his need to regain his lost honor. According to the Renaissance theory, honor is the respect or recognition given to a gentleman as his birthright by all aristocrats. Called home from Paris, Laertes can learn only that his father has died suddenly in a mysterious way and that he has been buried hurriedly and secretly, with no monument over him (213-215). For an aged councillor high in the favor of the King, this is disgraceful treatment; and rumor whispers that Polonius must have committed some great blunder or treason (89-94).[40] Treason by a father dishonors his children. Laertes cannot wait for time to reveal the truth; delay will nearly ruin his prospects for marriage and a career. He must demand redress at once. But the chief source of honor in the realm, King Claudius, is also the probable instigator of Polonius' assassination and therefore Laertes's chief enemy. In addition, the King's position makes it difficult, though not impossible, to challenge him. Laertes's obstacles to satisfaction seem almost as great as Hamlet's.

Therefore, Laertes takes what he thinks the only practical way of getting restitution of his honor; he gathers a faction and threatens rebellion (101). By this means he can demand punishment for the slayer, a public funeral for Polonius, and proper compensation for the injury to his own honor (for instance, a gift of large estates). In only a few days at most he has chosen his course and driven ahead in it, to the point where we meet him in this scene.

His immediate raising of the insurrection contrasts, temperamentally, to Hamlet's painful reflection, struggle against apathy, loss of will, and use of prolonged observation and the test of "The Mouse-Trap." Laertes, we shall see in the remainder of the play, is a man of quick, violent emotions—in this scene, furious anger and convulsive grief. The emotion pours out in extravagant words.

> To hell, allegiance! Vows [*of loyalty*] to the blackest devil!
> I dare damnation . . . only I'll be reveng'd
> Most throughly for my father. . . .
> O heat [*of passion*], dry up my brains! Tears seven times salt
> Burn out the sense and virtue of mine eye! (131-136, 154-155)

But obviously he is capable of dangerous action, also.

When Laertes bursts through the guards with his mob, Claudius and Gertrude show their best quality. Gertrude rushes between the men and clings to Laertes's sword arm, thus testifying to her love and courage. Claudius too evinces courage and self-possession, for he recovers his dominance over Laertes by only a few speeches; and this he accomplishes in spite of a heavy handicap, the presence of Gertrude, which prevents him from telling Laertes about Hamlet's killing of Polonius and Hamlet's doom. The re-entrance of Ophelia plunges Laertes into an agony and perhaps enables Claudius more readily to gain ascendancy.

SCENE 6. This, of course, is sheer mechanism of plot. Horatio presumably moves downstage to read the letter to the audience, out of the sailor's hearing.

SCENE 7. This scene of villainous intrigue is salted with several dramatic ironies. Claudius, in private talk with Laertes, has revealed a reason for Hamlet's enmity to the King, his slaying of

A Commentary on the Action / Act IV

Polonius, and his pretended or actual madness. The reason is surely ambition. He is on the point of telling about the Prince's fate in England and what can be done to restore Laertes's honor, when a messenger delivers Hamlet's letter promising his return. Although by this coincidence Claudius just escapes revealing his treachery, he is confounded by the news, which tells him he now has *two* malcontents to dispose of. But his agile mind is best revealed in this scene. At once he begins to sound and evaluate Laertes as a weapon to kill Hamlet. In the long conversation in 62-125, which obviously serves as exposition and preparation for the last scene of the play, one feels that Claudius is studying Laertes's reliability as a partner in intrigue. Having decided to use him, Claudius outlines the plot, and Laertes surpasses the King's hopes by his willingness to use treachery to regain his honor. All seems going well. But now comes Gertrude with the news of Ophelia's suicide. Laertes rushes out, weeping; and for the second time within an hour, fate has tried to blow up Claudius's careful plot.

Gertrude's description of Ophelia's drowning is a lyric passage of pathos. Gertrude is depersonalized for a few moments and speaks with a poetic eloquence which she has shown no signs of possessing elsewhere in the play. But the fact that she is a woman helps; the recital would have been much less appropriate in the mouth of a manservant or messenger. And Shakespeare wants to introduce the tender note of pathos because of the irony it will contribute to the Graveyard Scene that follows.

Act V

SCENE 1. A day, perhaps, elapses between Ophelia's suicide and her unceremonious burial. It cannot be proved from the play that Claudius has hastened the funeral, a risky thing to do considering the soreness of Laertes's feelings; but probably Claudius wishes that the funeral may be over before Hamlet arrives, in order to allow his plot to develop uncomplicated. But in this hope Claudius is frustrated.

In a play full of good theater probably no scene is richer in appeal than this one. Yet considering its nearness to the bloody catastrophe, one must say that this scene is a strange, provocative prelude to the ending. Here is a unique mingling of dramatic interests—satiric farce and macabre meditation blended, followed by intense irony and grotesque violence. Throughout the whole scene, the hero acts in ironic ignorance of his situation.

The two Gravediggers enter with their equipment and move to the edge of the larger trap door, in the outer stage.[41] But they are comically lazy and must finish an argument, leaning on their tools, before one of them sets to work (68). They are the sexton (First Gravedigger) and his younger helper; and possibly they are more like the workers of Holy Trinity Parish in Stratford than like Londoners. The sexton is a bit annoyed by an order from the pastor to hurry up and get this grave dug within a few hours— such haste just for a suicide who does not even belong in consecrated ground! He makes some caustic remarks about special favors that influence can get for aristocratic sinners. Finally, he peels off three or four jackets in succession,[42] steps onto the trap, and, as it slowly descends, swings his pick, then wields his shovel. He sings jerkily, remembering something of the tune, few of the words, of a popular lovesong of forty years before.

Presumably no one in the audience, realizing from the Gravediggers' talk that the grave is Ophelia's, will wonder why Hamlet and Horatio have chosen to approach the castle of Elsinore through the churchyard. It will be far more absorbing to relish the irony of Hamlet's witty discourses at this spot and to await the arrival of the funeral of his dead lover.[43]

A Commentary on the Action / Act V

Hamlet's recent escape from death has perhaps confirmed that more normal state of mind that we detected in the last soliloquy (IV.4.32-66). It is partly just curiosity that a gravedigger can sing at his task that draws him to the scene. Then too the wit and satire he utters in this scene have a gayer tone than anything he has said since his talk with the players. However, we need not forget that a melancholy man is often satiric, as well as habituated to thoughts of death. The meditations on the skulls, therefore, are at least appropriate for a melancholy man.

The passage of satire, though well blended with the macabre tone, probably seemed appropriate to Shakespeare because of the current literary vogue of satire (more or less directly imitated from Roman poets like Juvenal). The English vogue reached its height in 1599, but its echoes were heard in the drama for some years afterward. The figures of the politician, the courtier, the lawyer, and the painted lady appear traditionally in such satire. Yet underlying most of Hamlet's comments is a medieval theme that is more serious than the satiric one, that is, *de contemptu mundi*, the shortness of earthly gain, pleasure, and pride.

And so Hamlet moralizes with wit and pathos, at great length, and finally concludes with a jingling rhyme on Imperial Caesar. As if to put his philosophy to some kind of ironic test, the body of Ophelia enters the stage.

The circumstances of this funeral have more than usual dramatic significance; we should stop to note them. Members of important families were usually buried under the floor of the church; Laertes is humiliated that this privilege is denied his sister, though interment even in the churchyard has evidently been permitted only because of Claudius's insistence (251). The funeral ceremony is humiliatingly short and crude. No Requiem Mass has been sung in the church, and the prayers at the graveside are shortened to a few phrases or omitted entirely (242, 246). Only one priest, instead of two or three with acolytes, accompanies the coffin. A bell offstage tolls a few times (257).[44] The coffin (apparently without its cover, at first) is lowered onto the trap; and this is the end of poor Ophelia's story. Laertes is agonized with shame and grief; Hamlet is pierced with shame at his complacent display of wit at this graveside a few moments before.

We sympathize with Laertes's feelings, but we have to condemn his theatrical display of them. His leaping into the grave is forgivable, but not his cursing of Hamlet or his ranting plea to be buried alive. Obviously, Hamlet's disgust with this extravagance mingles with other feelings to drive him forward, even to make him leap into the grave to outrant his denouncer. (The First Quarto edition of 1603 reveals this action, though the Second Quarto and Folio say nothing of it.)

When they have been dragged from the grave and separated, Hamlet continues to show his disgust by shouting even more grotesque exaggerations than Laertes has used. But let us not overlook the more important emotions whose disturbance makes him more a spectacle than Laertes has been. Presumably real grief for Ophelia, shock at her suicide, remorse for his being the cause —these passions augment the shame and disgust previously mentioned. Most critics say he is not assuming the antic disposition here; but certainly the spectators believe he is as mad as ever, and as dangerous (295, 308, 319). Mad or not, the Prince has treated Laertes with outrageous contempt. Laertes is too angry to speak; he reaches for his sword (295-296). But Claudius manages to suppress any violence for the moment. And now for Hamlet there can be only imprisonment or death. He has brought back in his pocket the documentary proof of Claudius's treachery; but his burst of passion has largely swept away any advantage that proof might have given him. The apathy of the melancholiac, or the morbid grief, has been replaced in Hamlet by emotions that appear more normal. But they have proved as treacherous as melancholy. His homecoming is not auspicious.

SCENE 2.   At this point in the action of many revenge tragedies, we find the hero secretly gathering his friends and henchmen and organizing the masque, the play, or other device which is to be the cover for an assault upon the oppressor. Even in the saga of Amlothi, the ultimate source of *Hamlet,* the hero, though acting alone, is the aggressor against his uncle. But Shakespeare's Prince characteristically spends most of his last scene in witty, philosophical talk, while Claudius takes the initiative against him. Hamlet is perhaps too noble a person to organize a plot against Claudius. When he says, *The interim is mine* (73), he is just as vague as he ever has been about how he proposes to kill Claudius; and probably if the interim were five years, the deed might not be done. But this may be unfair. At least Hamlet says that he has learned the value of rashness and indiscretion (6-9) and the reliance on some superhuman power rather than, presumably, human reason to carry him to his goal. The note of acquiescence

A Commentary on the Action / Act V

in whatever fate may send him, death or life, is to be found in 6-9, in 73-74, and more distinctly in 230-235. We may express Hamlet's attitude another way by saying that if he cannot plot cold-bloodedly even against Claudius, he has learned that by biding his time he can react intuitively, but successfully, against the attack of the enemy. Yet if his reaction fails and death must be his lot—*the readiness is all* (233).

Most of the conversation with Horatio (1-79) tells us what in real life we should expect Hamlet to have told Horatio yesterday, when Horatio met him approaching Elsinore. But it is told in so lively a way we do not think of that.

The interview with young Osric is a surprising episode of satiric comedy to find so close to the catastrophe. Osric is a caricature of the foppish courtier. In clothing, manners, and language he is preposterously affected. Hamlet calls him a water-fly because of his plumes and satins, a chough because he chatters like a magpie. After greeting Hamlet, he stands preening himself, combing his lovelock or his beard, while Hamlet comments on him to Horatio (83-90). Hamlet parodies his silly diction to the fellow's face, without arousing any resentment. Some critics have taken Osric rather seriously as an embodiment of imbecility which is part of the "rottenness" in Denmark. It seems more likely that Shakespeare introduced him partly to conform to the vogue of satire Ben Jonson launched in English drama, partly to serve the plot in a minor, but real, way.

He brings the news of the friendly wager Claudius has made with Laertes. After Hamlet's insults to Laertes at the grave-side, Hamlet should suspect he may become the victim of a collusion between Laertes and Claudius. But he does not, and possibly Hamlet's lack of suspicion here may be made more plausible to the audience because the evil challenge comes wrapped up in Osric's harmless silliness. Moreover, Hamlet's amusing, sharp satires against the fop may serve to divert the audience from a critical attitude toward Hamlet's gullibility. It should be noted, too, that the duel follows almost at once; there is almost no time for Hamlet to reflect on the situation.

It is not wholly consistent with Hamlet's condition of deep melancholy after the Ghost's visit that the prince should have practiced daily with the rapier (220-222). Such vigorous exercise is either the cause or the result of more normal physical and mental health than Hamlet seems to have during that space of eight or nine weeks. On the other hand, the fencing match must not be an easy victory for Laertes. The audience recall that in Act IV. 7 Claudius has repeated the Frenchman's praise of Laertes's extraordinary skill. Shakespeare, having more regard for dramatic truth than petty realism, deliberately prepares us for Hamlet's superiority in the fencing match by mentioning his zealous practice and confidence (compare also IV.7.103-106).

Although the phrase *laid on twelve for nine* (173) has not been well explained, the King's wager is clear. It is complimentary to Hamlet, for it assumes that the two fencers are almost equal, despite the fact that Laertes has spent months in Paris and has excelled in the best schools of fencing in Europe. Claudius bets that out of twelve bouts, Laertes will not win a majority that totals three more than Hamlet's total of wins. (Each bout with the rapiers is ended by a contestant's making a touch or hit.) For instance, if the score is Laertes 7, Hamlet 5, Claudius wins his bet; but if the score is Laertes 8, Hamlet 4, Claudius loses.

Probably a flourish is sounded while attendants set out the thrones of the King and Queen, cushions for the gentlemen who are to sit on the floor, a table with wine, and the foils and gauntlets.[45] Hamlet and Horatio stand aside downstage while the royal party enter and seat themselves, with Laertes standing close to the throne. Then Claudius calls Hamlet and joins his and Laertes's hands in a treacherous pretense of reconcilement. In a very rational, somewhat formal, but apparently sincere speech,[46] Hamlet apologizes for his insults to Laertes at the funeral. It is a little disturbing that he attributes his acts to madness, for we believe that in that scene he is neither mad nor pretending to be. But he certainly is excited to the point of seeming insane to the spectators. His explanation here is probably the only possible one, it is consistent with his antic disposition of the past months, and (though Hamlet is ignorant of this) it is made to two men who are not interested in reconcilement, but in his death. Laertes's answer is a formal, conditional acceptance of the apology, reserving the right to demand more satisfaction (i.e., a duel) if men learned in the code of honor, from whom Laertes is asking advice, inform him that nothing but a victory at arms can restore his honor. Laertes's behavior here is interesting, for it exemplifies the kind of conduct that a "gentleman" could use in the pursuit of honor. The slaying of Polonius and the public insults at Ophelia's funeral are outrages that fully justify Laertes (he believes) in the treacherous revenge he is about to take on Hamlet. However, he

A Commentary on the Action / Act V

will not stoop to the basest hypocrisy of pretending a renewed friendship with his enemy.[47]

Young Osric makes an appropriate umpire for the match. Being convinced of his naïveté, the audience is less inclined to suspect that he is an accomplice of the plotters; and in fact, he is not. None is needed; an accomplice might betray them. Because he is relatively inexperienced, Osric is dramatically the right referee, one who will not observe Laertes's sharp rapier and who will have difficulty separating the fencers when they get angry.

Almost all Shakespearian tragedies end with physical combat and with symbolic noises resounding through the theater. So with *Hamlet*. At the King's command, kettle drums roar, trumpets peal, and cannon boom from the "hut," aloft (285-289). Trumpets and cannon sound again after Hamlet's first hit (294) and his second (296). Distant drumming and cannonades make an obbligato for the death of Hamlet, the approach of Fortinbras, and the removal of the bodies. Though Shakespeare no doubt intends to create theatrical excitement just by crashing noises, he also profits here from both conventional and particular symbolism. Thunder, with its significance of supernatural power striking down evil, was symbolized in the Elizabethan theater by cannon shots; hence the present scene may gain solemnity by giving a parallel with thunder, significant of Divine intervention in this evil plot. There is also an ironic fitness in the cannon booms that accompany Claudius's last fatal carouse in this scene; they recall the cannonades that signalized his toasts, like a mockery of Hamlet, as the prince awaited the Ghost in I.4. Thus the play's beginning and end are united by symbolic sounds.

Drinker though he is, Claudius does not for a moment forget to forward the plot. He tries to clinch success at once by poison. His overeagerness ironically coöperates with Gertrude's appetite and results in disaster; she takes the cup of poisoned wine. He rises, intending to stay her hand—*too late* (303). Sick with horror, he falls silent. His last two speeches reveal his panic fear of punishment and a desperate desire to survive (319, 335). Though the villain has shown self-command, he has no fortitude.

In the duel, of three bouts, Hamlet wins the first two, and the third is a draw (312). Either at the beginning of the fourth bout or before it can begin, Laertes wounds Hamlet. The mechanics of the wounding and the exchange of weapons that follows have been explained in various ways. The Old Vic performance on television (ca. 1961) offers a convincing method for the business. When Osric calls the draw (312), Hamlet lowers his foil and turns away for a moment's rest allowed; Laertes lunges and wounds him in the back. Hamlet turns, in a fury, and after a half dozen thrusts, knocks Laertes's rapier to the floor. He picks it up, sees its sharp point, hands his own blunted weapon to Laertes, and then attacks and wounds him. Osric feebly attempts to halt the bout.

Perhaps Hamlet is bewildered by Gertrude's falling from her chair and by the pain of his own wound; but Laertes' words identify the King publicly as murderer, and Hamlet executes him without delay with the poisoned rapier. Though the King can call for help, he writhes in agony, and after trying to stand, falls back upon the throne, dying. Hamlet staggers to the table, takes the golden goblet of poisoned wine, and, seizing Claudius by the hair, turns up his face and dashes some of the wine on his mouth. It is a symbolic action only, for the King is unconscious. With the last of his strength Hamlet topples Claudius to the floor—*Follow my mother!*—and then with Horatio to support him, turns and seats himself on the throne of Denmark.

He is still clutching the poisoned cup; Horatio takes it from him. But when Horatio raises his arm to drink the dregs from it, Hamlet lunges, seizes his wrist, and spills the drops. When the Prince has spoken the painful phrases that commission his friend to clear Hamlet's good name, a far-off drum roll is heard, beating a march. Nearby is the crack of a volley of muskets. As Hamlet dies, the drums roll more and more loudly; they complete the crescendo as Fortinbras and the English Ambassador enter in procession. A long, silent pause of amazement climaxes the entrance as they see the dead Prince on his throne among the dead.

Probably the English Ambassador appears for the denouement because, since Fortinbras must now succeed to the throne of Denmark, and since England is a subject nation, his sovereignty over it too is confirmed by the presence of the Ambassador. Furthermore, at the end of a play Shakespeare tries not to leave anyone's fate in doubt; and so we hear the last of Rosencrantz and Guildenstern.

While Horatio at once begins his explanation of these bloody acts, soldiers carry off the bodies of Gertrude, Laertes, and Claudius. Then as the drums softly sound a funeral march, four captains place Hamlet's body on a stretcher and bear it out, while Fortinbras speaks a soldierlike eulogy. Then the slow drums thunder more loudly. Fortinbras, who has already asserted his right to kingship here, marches out with his party, and as the last soldier leaves, a volley of cannon fire reverberates on the empty stage with its empty throne.

To many critics it has seemed that the actual slaying of Claudius hardly fulfills a true conception of revenge as intended by the Ghost. The execution has a time and manner unanticipated by Hamlet and appears more or less accidental or perhaps Providential. But Hamlet does not seem to express any such idea in his dying speeches. His great regret is that he must die without time for justifying to the Danish public the killings he has done—in other words, without time for explanation of his life of the last three months. This explanation he must entrust to Horatio, whom he commands to absent himself *from felicity* (the afterlife) to tell the story. Hamlet's sorrow may imply a regret that he cannot fulfill the Ghost's sequel command, to rule Denmark after Claudius's death. But that Hamlet feels himself to have seriously failed in the obligation laid on him—this idea cannot be properly inferred from what he says.

Then if he is convicted of failure, it is we who convict him. But perhaps the question of whether he has accomplished a proper revenge is largely irrelevant. An analysis of Hamlet's tragedy may be better guided by trying to answer such questions as these: (1) What are the evils in Hamlet's life (keeping within the two to three months' scope of the play)? Certainly there are evils within his own character and evils outside him. There are evils of his doing and of others' creating. This question opens up philosophical aspects as well as details of the action. (2) What is the source of these evils? We must confine ourselves to the period in Hamlet's life comprised in the play and avoid the fallacy of ranging far into the past. What he is in the play partly has its origin in the past; but it is best to accept the data given about him and his situation at the beginning without theorizing freely about how they came to be; for such theorizing leads to loss of a sense of relative values among the elements of the play and tends to make the interpreter forget the matrix of dramatic conventions and audience reactions on which Shakespeare depended as he wrote a play. (3) Do the evils overwhelm and defeat the hero? This question very obviously seems philosophical; but like the two preceding, it should fundamentally be much controlled by the truth of dramatic history that scholarship can give us. As but one passage where this control is needed: What is the significance of the military honors Fortinbras pays to Hamlet at his burial? Is the dramatist using a conventional device to impart to the hero a degree of dignity lost through too many scenes of frustration and antic disposition? Or is the device an incongruous tribute paid by an unreflective man of action to the man of thought who has ended by being able to act only instinctively?

The knowledge required to answer all questions about *Hamlet* has not yet been accumulated, and all of it may never be at any one person's command. There is some comfort in this fact. There is more for you in the fact that *Hamlet* may be studied hard many times without losing its fascination.

A Summary of the Action

ACT I

SCENE 1. At midnight Bernardo replaces Francisco as sentry before the castle of Elsinore. Bernardo is accompanied by Marcellus, an officer, and Horatio, a student. Bernardo and Marcellus have invited Horatio to come and determine the nature of an apparition which looks like the dead King Hamlet of Denmark, and which has appeared to them twice the preceding night. The Ghost soon appears. It does not answer Horatio's questions, but walks across the yard, and disappears. Horatio tells about the duel which this dead King fought with a Norwegian noble, Fortinbras, who was slain by the King. Young Fortinbras, son of the defeated noble, has been preparing an invasion of Danish territory to recover the lands his father lost by defeat. But the dead King's brother, King Claudius, is preparing to outfit an army to repel young Fortinbras.

The Ghost of King Hamlet returns, again refuses to speak, and disappears whence it came. The three observers agree that this visitation must be reported to Prince Hamlet, son of the dead King.

SCENE 2. Next morning at a Council of State King Claudius thanks his Danish nobles for the approval they have given to his marriage to Queen Gertrude, widow of King Hamlet. She has been a widow not quite two months. (Claudius has succeeded his brother on the throne by winning support of Polonius, an old, influential nobleman; for Denmark is an elective monarchy. By this maneuver Claudius has excluded Prince Hamlet, a student at the University of Wittenberg, from succeeding his father.) Claudius tells his Council of State that he has taken measures to frustrate young Fortinbras's threatened invasion. Claudius dispatches two ambassadors, Voltimand and Cornelius, to the King of Norway, a feeble old man, to demand that the King forbid any military effort by Fortinbras and disband his troops. Then Claudius turns to minor matters and grants permission to Laertes,

Polonius' son, to return to Paris for further tutoring in arms and social graces. But the King refuses Hamlet's wish to return to the University of Wittenberg. It is clear that Claudius is displeased that Hamlet still wears mourning for his dead father, despite the wedding festivities now in progress. He rebukes Hamlet for his unreasonable grief and professes to want to keep the Prince where Claudius can cheer him up. Gertrude also disapproves Hamlet's request, and Hamlet has to submit to disappointment.

When the Council is over, in soliloquy Hamlet reveals he is in a dangerous state of suicidal melancholy, chiefly caused by his mother's hasty, incestuous marriage to a man loathsome to Hamlet. Horatio, Marcellus, and Bernardo interrupt the Prince's meditation; we learn that Horatio has been a friend of Hamlet's at Wittenberg. Astounded by the news of the Ghost, Hamlet agrees to meet Horatio and Marcellus at midnight at the sentry's post before the castle. By himself again, Hamlet surmises that the Ghost may reveal a dangerous plot against Denmark or perhaps against the Prince's life.

SCENE 3. That afternoon Laertes is all packed and ready to leave. In saying farewell to his sister Ophelia, he gives her lengthy advice, telling her to discourage the wooing of her suitor, Prince Hamlet, who is too far above her in rank. Then, in turn, Polonius gives Laertes a long lecture about how to live prudently among gentlemen in France; next, Polonius turns to Ophelia and forbids her to meet or communicate with Hamlet any more. She promises to obey.

SCENE 4. At midnight upon the platform (yard) before the castle Hamlet, Horatio, and Marcellus nervously await the apparition and talk of the Danish habit of drunkenness, shamefully exemplified in King Claudius. The night air is shaken by trumpet calls and cannonades which signalize each cupful the King drinks off. The Ghost appears and without answering Hamlet's questions beckons him to follow to a private place. Against his friends' wishes, Hamlet follows the Ghost.

SCENE 5. Alone with Hamlet, the Ghost at last speaks and relates events which shock and sicken Hamlet: (1) King Hamlet's death was not natural, as reported, but by poison treacherously poured in the King's ears while he slept; the murderer was his brother Claudius. (2) By this unexepected death King

A Summary of the Action / Act II

Hamlet was sent to judgment, unprepared by contrition or the graces infused through confession, the Eucharist, and anointing by the priest. Consequently, the King's punishment in Purgatory is to be a long and horrible one, both in torment of flame and of walking by night in the scenes of his sins. (3) While the King still lived, Claudius seduced Queen Gertrude. She was guilty of both incest and adultery before her husband's death.

The Ghost calls on Hamlet to revenge the murder, but forbids him to punish Gertrude for her crimes. Almost insane with the horror of these revelations, Hamlet promises revenge. The Ghost exits.

Horatio and Marcellus now come upon Hamlet; but he dares not tell what he has learned from the Ghost. He swears them to secrecy about the Ghost's visit, using the cross of his sword-hilt, as the Ghost speaks from underground to terrify them. Hamlet warns them that in public he will pretend to be mad.

ACT II

SCENE 1. About two months have elapsed. Laertes is still in Paris; Polonius dispatches money to him by a manservant, Reynaldo. In fear and distress, Ophelia comes to tell her father about a very strange visit Hamlet has paid to her chamber; he came and went without a word, his clothing disheveled, his face pale and staring. Polonius at once decides Hamlet has become mad with frustrated love-longing, i.e., love-melancholy. He decides to inform the King.

SCENE 2. A few days before this, Claudius has become so disturbed about Hamlet's changed appearance and deep melancholia (his melancholy before the Ghost's message has been vastly increased since then) that he has sent for two young men who were Hamlet's friends, perhaps before the Prince went to Wittenberg. They are Rosencrantz and Guildenstern, two gentlemen who hope to rise in the favor of the King. Claudius asks them to renew their friendship with Hamlet and find out what secret desire or resentment is causing his melancholy, then report it to the King so that he may remedy it. The two young spies are remarkably alike in character and in speech, probably also in costume on the stage.

Polonius reports to Claudius that the two ambassadors to Norway have returned and also that he himself has discovered the cause of Hamlet's *lunacy.* So important is the mystery of Hamlet to Claudius that he would rather hear about it first; but Polonius insists on the results of the mission to Norway first. That report is excellent: Fortinbras has submitted to his angry uncle, the King of Norway, and has promised on oath never to attack Denmark. His King, well-pleased, has given him permission to make a campaign against the Poles, and Fortinbras would like permission to march across Danish territory for this purpose. Claudius announces that he will consider this request soon.

Now it is Polonius's chance to hold the floor, and he talks at length, pompously, about madness and Hamlet's love-sickness, reading a letter in verse that Ophelia has received earlier from the Prince. Queen Gertrude rather thinks love may be the source of Hamlet's crazed behavior, but Claudius continues to be skeptical. So Polonius offers to bring Claudius where he and Polonius may watch and listen as Hamlet talks with Ophelia, the Prince being unaware of witnesses. In that situation Hamlet will betray the overmastering passion that has taken the form of melancholia. The King agrees to this plan.

Just then Hamlet enters the room; the others leave, and Polonius greets the Prince. Hamlet's response is mad talk, the *antic disposition* which he mentioned to Horatio, but which we have not seen thus far (for we have not seen Hamlet since the Ghost's visit with him). In riddling words Hamlet warns Polonius that his daughter may become the victim of a seducer; then he insults the councilor by describing old age in ugly terms. As Polonius leaves, baffled, Rosencrantz and Guildenstern come seeking the Prince. Hamlet warmly welcomes them; but their evasive manner about why they have sought him out arouses his suspicion, which soon becomes certainty. They deal clumsily with what they think is a mad mind, and their answers reveal that they suspect a frustrated desire for the throne may have created Hamlet's melancholy. Hamlet does not say outright this is the cause, but broadly hints that it is, and plainly tells them he knows they are sent by the King and Queen to spy on him. His disgust with them prompts him to describe his misanthropy in a famous Apostrophe on Man. To change the subject, Rosencrantz announces that the actors from "the city" have arrived and would like to perform for Hamlet (for a fee).

The Prince is delighted; it appears he has known them for long and enjoys the drama. Rosencrantz describes the rivalry be-

A Summary of the Action / Act III

tween the companies of men actors and those of boy actors, who have enjoyed a sudden vogue of great popularity over the adult companies, forcing the men to leave the city and go on tour. Polonius now returns with the belated announcement that the actors have come. Hamlet ridicules him even more broadly than before.

As the players come in, Hamlet gives them an enthusiastic welcome. At once he calls for a set speech, an heroical, rather old-fashioned description of Pyrrhus's slaughter of Priam, king of Troy. In spite of interruptions by Polonius, who does not relish it, the player manages to work up so much feeling as to weep during his recitation. Afterwards, when Polonius has gone, Hamlet employs the company to produce a play called "The Murder of Gonzago" tomorrow evening before the whole court; and they agree to insert at one place a dozen or more lines of Hamlet's own, which he will give them tonight. Rosencrantz and Guildenstern see nothing remarkable in this.

Alone again, Hamlet speaks his second major soliloquy. The emotionalism of the player in the Pyrrhus speech makes Hamlet contrast his own apathy, which is characteristic of profound melancholy, and also his failure to act, to engage in his revenge. Hamlet tries to account for the two months of listless, shameful inertia that have passed since he talked with the Ghost. He denies that he is afraid of the danger involved; then abruptly decides he must indeed be a coward. He whips up a semblance of fury against Claudius, then abruptly abandons the futility of the shouting and finds satisfaction in the play of tomorrow night. That play will re-enact the murder of King Hamlet, and if Claudius betrays his guilt by a single grimace of pain, the Prince knows what to do.

ACT III

SCENE 1. Next day the King and Queen meet with Rosencrantz and Guildenstern to learn what the young men have discovered; they have to report, however, that he has been too crafty for them and that they have learned nothing yet. The King is relieved to hear that Hamlet is interested in the players, and willingly consents to attend the play. When all the rest except Claudius have gone, Polonius stations Ophelia where Hamlet will meet her in his walk, telling her to read in a book of religious meditation which he gives her. The King feels a pang of shame at this hypocrisy and, in a short aside, confesses the heavy guilt he feels. Then Polonius and Claudius withdraw to a hiding place on the upper stage overlooking the meeting place.

Hamlet comes in meditating on suicide (*To be or not to be*). The soliloquy considers suicide as a general problem, not as Hamlet's in particular. Hamlet concludes that many more people would commit suicide, were it not for fear of the unknown future that lies (or may lie) beyond the grave. At the end of the soliloquy Hamlet observes Ophelia reading, or pretending to read, what is obviously a religious book. If he does not immediately suspect her of pretense, he does so very soon, and his *antic disposition* grows more violent as he talks with her. She returns some jewels he has given her, thus further angering him by her subservience to her father. He condemns both men and women for their lust and orders Ophelia to keep her virtue by getting to a nunnery (this episode is called the Nunnery Scene). He obviously suspects that she has been "planted" there by her father, probably with Claudius's connivance, and that both are watching. He ends with a tirade against women. Then he exits.

Ophelia is weeping with grief at his distraction. She contrasts the former Hamlet with the ruined one she has just tried to converse with. Formerly this Prince was the ideal gentleman accomplished in all graces, a courtier, soldier, scholar. Now he raves.

Claudius, however, has seen deeper than Polonius and Ophelia and believes that Hamlet's talk *was not like madness*. Furthermore, whatever the underlying passion, it is not love. Now the King much more keenly suspects danger to himself. He tells Polonius he will deport Hamlet to England in the hope that change of scene will be good for him. Polonius cannot veto the plan, but obstinately maintains that love is the cause and that if Gertrude will cross-examine Hamlet, while Polonius again eavesdrops, the true cause of madness will be found. Claudius consents to this repetition of the device of catching the madman offguard while he is worked on by the sympathy of his mother.

SCENE 2. In the early evening Hamlet meets the players, to make sure they have included his dozen or more lines; he tells them how to speak the passage, and then delivers a lecture on acting in general. Bidding the actors get ready, he talks with Horatio alone, frankly telling how much he loves and admires his friend. Then he asks Horatio, who by now has been informed

A Summary of the Action / Act III

of King Hamlet's murder, to help Hamlet detect signs of Claudius's guilt during the play.

The King and Queen, Polonius, Ophelia, Rosencrantz and Guildenstern and other attendants enter the great hall and seat themselves to watch "The Murder of Gonzago" (as yet the King is unaware of its title or theme). Hamlet sits at Ophelia's feet, torments her with indecent remarks, and also acts his antic part with Polonius, the King, and the Queen. He frequently interrupts the opening of the play with annoying remarks which grow more pointed at Claudius as the plot progresses. He tells the King the title is "The Mouse-Trap."

The play itself is preceded by two overtures, a dumb-show which pantomimes the theme (apparently of the first act) and a prologue, which is of little value and only asks the audience's tolerance. The play itself begins very slowly, the situation being developed through long speeches. It concerns Gonzago, Duke of Vienna, whose wife Baptista protests she loves him; but when the Duke is murdered in his sleep by his nephew,[1] Baptista promptly accepts him as her lover.

But King Claudius cannot endure to see all of this; when the nephew poisons his sleeping victim, Claudius rises, calls for torches, and hurries away to his chamber. The play is cut short. Hamlet is wildly exultant at the success of his scheme. Presently Rosencrantz and Guildenstern bring him word that the King and Queen are angry with him for his rude behavior at the play and that the Queen wishes to talk with him. Before he obeys, Hamlet plays his mad part with the two spies and contemptuously ridicules them and Polonius. Alone, he resolves to rebuke his mother, but not to harm her.

SCENE 3. (This is the Prayer Scene.) Realizing now that Hamlet knows about his father's murder, Claudius commands Rosencrantz and Guildenstern to prepare to escort Hamlet to England the next day. Polonius enters to tell the King he will conceal himself in Gertrude's chamber and listen to Hamlet's talk with his mother. When he is alone, the King kneels to pray, overcome by guilt for the murder; but, recognizing that he is not willing to give up the fruits of his sins, he admits that he does not hate the sins enough to be forgiven. While he is speaking these thoughts aloud, Hamlet, unobserved, passes behind him, sees him, and pauses. It is a unique opportunity to accomplish the revenge; but

Hamlet cannot bring himself to strike. He says he will rather kill Claudius when the King is in some sinful act, and thus send him to Hell. Hamlet goes on, to Gertrude's chamber.

SCENE 4. (This is the Closet Scene.) Polonius, with Gertrude's consent, hides himself behind the arras. Hamlet enters highly excited by the events of the last two hours and intent on punishing his mother verbally as well as determining whether she was an accomplice in King Hamlet's murder. Hamlet's violence of words and gestures frightens the Queen into calling for help; Polonius, in a panic, cries for help; and Hamlet, supposing that it is the King, draws his rapier and stabs through the arras, killing Polonius. Hence Gertrude decides Hamlet is a maniac.

Hamlet tries to accomplish his intended purpose, and lashes his mother with contempt for her lustfulness (but he does not reveal that he knows of her adultery; for he is now convinced she is ignorant of the murder of her husband). Gertrude appears ashamed of her lustful, incestuous marriage. But now Hamlet is interrupted by the Ghost, who comes to remind the Prince of his duty of revenge and to urge him to be considerate of his mother. Unable to see the Ghost, Gertrude has another proof of Hamlet's insanity. When the Ghost has gone, Hamlet exhorts her to give up intercourse with Claudius; but she does not promise this forthrightly. Hamlet drags out the body of Polonius.

ACT IV

SCENE 1. A few moments later, Gertrude reports Hamlet's violent insanity and the death of Polonius to the King. When Claudius tells her Hamlet must go to England, she cannot object. Rosencrantz and Guildenstern are sent to bring Polonius's body into the royal chapel, to await a hasty funeral.

SCENE 2. Rosencrantz and Guildenstern cannot get from Hamlet any inkling about where he has hidden the corpse. In his antic disposition he even plays hide-and-seek with them.

SCENE 3. In soliloquy Claudius regrets that he cannot execute Hamlet, but the Prince is too much loved by the people.

Hamlet is brought in by Rosencrantz, Guildenstern, and guards. The Prince gives crazy answers to Claudius's questions until he

A Summary of the Action / Act IV

thinks the King may order torture or imprisonment; then he tells where he has hidden the corpse. Claudius tells Hamlet (what the Prince has by some means already learned) that he must go to England. When Hamlet has gone to prepare, Claudius informs Rosencrantz and Guildenstern that the departure must be this very night. In soliloquy the King reveals that his letters to the English King command the instant death of Hamlet on his arrival. (England is at this time subject to Denmark.)

SCENE 4. Next day, Hamlet and his guard observe Fortinbras as the Norwegian hero with a force of a few hundreds marches toward Poland to gain possession of a *little patch of ground*. It is a desperate venture. In the fourth major soliloquy Hamlet compares this heroism for honor's sake with his own inertia about seeking revenge for a mother seduced, a father murdered, a throne lost. He renews his resolve, then journeys on toward the port, and England.

SCENE 5. About three days after Hamlet's departure, Ophelia has lost her mind under the stress of grief for her father, murdered by her former lover and buried hastily and secretly. The King and Queen are depressed by her pathetic madness when she visits them and more so by the dangerous behavior of Laertes, who has come from Paris and listened to malicious rumors about the mysterious death of his father.

In fact, Laertes has gathered a faction of malcontents and now breaks through the royal guard to confront Claudius and Gertrude with a demand to know the facts about Polonius's death. Claudius has just promised to tell him everything when Ophelia enters; and Laertes now first learns of her madness. His grief increases his determination to have satisfaction for his father's death. Claudius again promises it.

SCENE 6. Meantime Horatio receives a letter from Hamlet bringing the surprising news that pirates have captured him and are preparing to release him in Denmark if he will obtain them a certain favor—perhaps commissions as privateers. Horatio is to meet Hamlet after he lands.

SCENE 7. The King has told Laertes that mad Hamlet slew his father; Claudius justifies his deporting Hamlet, instead of executing him, on the grounds that the Queen and the people love the

Prince. Because Laertes is still determined on revenge, Claudius is about to tell him of Hamlet's doom in England when Hamlet's letter is delivered to Claudius informing him briefly that Hamlet is back on Danish soil and will present himself to the King tomorrow.

Claudius must immediately initiate a new method of disposing of Hamlet. For this purpose he decides to utilize Laertes's hatred, and he easily gets the young man's approval of a plan to engage Hamlet in a friendly match with blunted rapiers, in which Laertes shall stab the Prince with a sharp rapier covertly provided. Laertes improves on the plan by proposing to poison the rapier tip, and Claudius will ensure success by poisoning a cup of wine to be offered Hamlet for refreshment.

The Queen interrupts their conference to bring the sad news that mad Ophelia, while attempting to hang wreathes of flowers on the branches of a willow beside the river, has fallen in the water and drowned. Laertes's passion of grief seems to Claudius to threaten the control he has just regained over the young man.

ACT V

SCENE 1. The next day a sexton and his helper are digging Ophelia's grave in the churchyard when Hamlet and Horatio pass by. Surprised to hear the sexton singing, and ignorant of who is to be buried, Hamlet philosophizes over the skulls the gravedigger unearths. But a funeral procession approaches; it includes the King and Queen and Laertes. Hamlet and Horatio stand aside unobserved. The ceremony is painfully short and simple. Grieving Laertes is so offended by the bare formalities that he leaps into the grave and calls on the spectators to bury him with his wretched sister. Shocked to hear that Ophelia has killed herself, and disgusted by Laertes's theatricalism in his grief, Hamlet comes forward and leaps into the grave, ranting more loudly than Laertes. The brother is infuriated by the mockery, and tries to throttle him. They are separated and drawn from the grave. Hamlet continues a cruel satire of Laertes's ranting, then walks away. Though he intended no pretense of madness, the spectators are convinced that he is as crazed as he was before his departure.

SCENE 2. Hamlet tells Horatio how, when he was on shipboard, filled with a premonition of danger, he got up in the night

A Summary of the Action / Act V

and stole the packet of Claudius's letters from his guardians' bag. Opening it, he discovered the King's order for his death. Being a good penman, Hamlet rewrote the letters to order the immediate death of Rosencrantz and Guildenstern, sealed them with his father's signet, and replaced them in the bag. Those two young men courted that disaster when they chose to mingle in the quarrel between Hamlet and Claudius. Now Hamlet has a little time before the King will hear of their deaths and order the Prince to be beheaded for treasonous murder.

Osric, a foppish, silly young gallant, comes to bring Hamlet word about a wager the King has made. Hamlet ridicules the courtier's affected speech for a while, but at length learns from him that Claudius has made a large bet that Laertes cannot beat Hamlet by a three-point advantage in twelve bouts with the rapier. As Hamlet suspects no treachery and has been practicing fencing regularly for two months, he thinks the bet a reasonable one and agrees to the match. But he speaks of an ominous disquiet *about my heart*. Yet he is resigned to what may come.

The King, Queen, and attendants take their places to watch. Claudius calls Hamlet to the throne and places Laertes's hand in Hamlet's, as a plea for reconciliation. Hamlet apologizes to Laertes with seeming sincerity, the only doubtful aspect of his statement being that he blames his madness for the insult he has offered his *brother*. Laertes accepts the apology conditionally, reserving the right to demand further satisfaction if the experts in laws of honor shall tell him that he must. Hamlet seems to have anticipated such a reserved response.

Osric is master at arms and umpire of the match. He has a box of rapiers which he has not examined just before the match, for somehow Laertes has managed to place a sharp and poisoned one at the bottom of the pile. Choosing after Hamlet, Laertes tries one or two and finally extricates the deadly weapon. With false joviality the King drinks to Hamlet, and according to his custom, drums roll, trumpets peal, and cannon bellow as he drains the cup.

Hamlet wins the first bout, and Claudius prematurely urges Hamlet to quench his thirst with a large cup of wine in which a pearl (i.e., poison) has been dropped. Not yet needing refreshment, Hamlet sets the cup on a table near the throne. He wins the second bout, and as the fencers rest a few minutes, Gertrude takes Hamlet's cup and toasts his success. The King is horrified. The third bout is a draw. Laertes is exasperated at his poor showing and impatient for the kill. When Hamlet lowers his foil at the judgment of "Draw," Laertes wounds him. Enraged, Hamlet attacks him and after several thrusts knocks Laertes's rapier to the floor. Picking it up, he discovers the sharp tip, offers his own blunted weapon to Laertes, and renews the fight. As the Queen falls half-fainting from the anguish of the poison, Hamlet runs Laertes through the body.

The Queen cries out to Hamlet that she has been poisoned. For a moment Hamlet is bewildered; but Laertes, who is now repentant on the threshold of death, tells Hamlet that the Prince also is fatally poisoned—*the King's to blame.* Hamlet turns and stabs the King. Then from the table he takes the cup still half full of poisoned wine and dashes most of it into Claudius's gasping mouth. But Claudius dies a moment later from the wound. Feeling the chill of death in his nerves, Hamlet topples Claudius's body from the throne and sinks into the seat. He asks Horatio to tell the world the truth behind his apparent madness and this slaughter. But Horatio wishes to join his friend in death and raises the poisoned cup to drink. Hamlet manages to twist the cup from his grasp and spill the dregs of wine.

Faraway drums begin to sound a march that gradually approaches. A shot is fired offstage. A messenger brings word that Fortinbras, just arrived victoriously from Poland, has fired a greeting to the approaching ambassadors from England. As the drum beats grow louder, Hamlet publicly approves Fortinbras as next king of Denmark—his successor, for Hamlet has been King for a few minutes. Now he dies. The drummers usher in Fortinbras, the English Ambassador, and their troops. Horatio steps forward to explain the grisly scene a little and to promise to explain it in full when the bodies have been laid in state. Fortinbras summons the nobility of Denmark to hear his claim to the throne, for he is distantly related to the royal family. The bodies are removed; last of all, Hamlet's is carried by four captains, to the drumming of a military march, after which the boom of cannon ends the play. Hamlet will receive a soldier's funeral.

A Sampling of *Hamlet* Criticism

For very recent essays and books on *Hamlet* you should consult the annual bibliographies published in *Shakespeare Quarterly* and *Shakespeare Survey*. Almost all the following passages are short excerpts from essays or books.

—from Sir Thomas Hanmer's, *Some Remarks on the Tragedy of Hamlet, Prince of Denmark,* 1736.

"To speak Truth, our Poet, by keeping too close to the Groundwork of his Plot, has fallen into an Absurdity; for there appears no Reason at all in Nature, why the young Prince did not put the Usurper to Death as soon as possible, especially as Hamlet is represented as a Youth so brave, and so careless of his own life. . . . The Case indeed is this: Had Hamlet gone naturally to work, as we could suppose such a Prince to do in parallel Circumstances, there would have been an End of our Play. The Poet therefore was obliged to delay his Hero's Revenge; but then he should have contrived some good Reason for it."

—from Samuel Johnson, editor, *The Plays of William Shakespeare,* 1765.

"General Observation. If the dramas of Shakespeare were to be characterized each by the particular excellence which distinguishes it from the rest, we must allow the tragedy of *Hamlet* the praise of variety. The incidents are so numerous that the argument of the play would make a long tale. The scenes are interchangeably diversified with merriment and solemnity; with merriment that includes judicious and instructive observations, and solemnity not strained by poetical violence above the natural sentiments of man. New characters appear from time to time in continual succession, exhibiting various forms of life and particular modes of conversation. The pretended madness of Hamlet causes much mirth, the mournful distraction of Ophelia fills the heart with tenderness, and every personage produces the effect intended, from the apparition that in the first act chills the blood with horror to the fop in the last that exposes affectation to just contempt.

"The conduct [*plot*] is perhaps not wholly secure against objections. The action is indeed for the most part in continual progression, but there are some scenes which neither forward nor retard it. Of the feigned madness of Hamlet there appears no adequate cause, for he does nothing which he might not have done with the reputation of sanity. He plays the madman most when he treats Ophelia with so much rudeness, which seems to be useless and wanton cruelty.

"Hamlet is, through the whole play, rather an instrument than an agent. After he has, by the stratagem of the play, convicted the king, he makes no attempt to punish him, and his death is at last effected by an incident which Hamlet has no part in producing.

"The catastrophe is not very happily produced; the exchange of weapons is rather an expedient of necessity than a stroke of art. A scheme might easily have been formed to kill Hamlet with the dagger, and Laertes with the bowl.

"The poet is accused of having shown little regard to poetical justice and may be charged with equal neglect of poetical probability. The apparition left the regions of the dead to little purpose; the revenge which he demands is not obtained but by the death of him that was required to take it; and the gratification which would arise from the destruction of an usurper and a murderer is abated by the untimely death of Ophelia, the young, the beautiful, the harmless, and the pious."

—from William Richardson's *Essays on Shakespeare's Dramatic Characters,* 1784.

"In the conduct, however, which [Hamlet] displays, in the progress of the tragedy, he appears irresolute and indecisive; he accordingly engages in enterprises in which he fails; he discovers reluctance to perform actions, which, we think, need no hesitation; he proceeds to violent outrage, where the occasion does not seem to justify violence; he appears jocular where his situation is most serious and alarming; he uses subterfuges not consistent with an ingenuous mind; and he expresses sentiments not only immoral, but inhuman.

"This charge is heavy; yet every reader, and every audience, have hitherto taken part with Hamlet . . . Let us enquire, therefore, whether those particulars which have given such offense, may not be considered as the infirmities of a mind constituted like that of Hamlet. . . .

A Sampling of Hamlet Criticism

"Surely such disorder of mind, in characters like that of Hamlet, though not amounting to actual madness, yet exhibiting reason in extreme perplexity, and even trembling on the brink of madness, is not unusual. Meantime, Hamlet was fully sensible how strange those involuntary improprieties must appear to others: he was conscious he could not suppress them; he knew he was surrounded with spies; and was justly apprehensive, lest his suspicion or purposes be discovered. But how are these consequences to be prevented? By counterfeiting an insanity which in part exists. . . .

"You ask me, why he did not kill the Usurper? And I answer, because he was at that instant irresolute. This irresolution arose from the inherent principles of his constitution, and is to be accounted natural: it arose from virtuous, or at least from amiable sensibility, and therefore cannot be blamed. His sense of justice, or his feelings of tenderness, in a moment when his violent emotions were not excited, overcame his resentment. But you will urge the inconsistency of this account, with the inhuman sentiments he expresses:

> Up, sword, and know thou a more horrid hent:
> When he is drunk, asleep, or in his rage, etc.
> Then trip him up, etc.

"In reply to this difficulty, and it is not inconsiderable, I will venture to affirm, that these are not his real sentiments. There is nothing in the whole character of Hamlet that justifies such savage enormity."

—from S. T. Coleridge's, *Coleridge's Writings on Shakespeare,* 1811-1827.

"Hamlet's character is the prevalence of the abstracting and generalizing habit over the practical. He does not want courage, skill, will or opportunity, but every incident sets him thinking; . . . I have a smack of Hamlet myself, if I may say so. . . .

"In Hamlet I conceive [Shakespeare] to have wished to exemplify the moral necessity of a due balance between our attention to outward objects and our meditation on inward thoughts—a due balance between the real and the imaginary world. In Hamlet this balance does not exist—his thoughts, images, and fancy being far more vivid than his perceptions, and his very perceptions instantly passing thro' the medium of his contemplations, and acquiring as they pass a form and color not naturally their own. Hence great, enormous, intellectual activity, and consequent proportionate aversion to real action, with all its symptoms and accompanying qualities. . . .

". . . Endless reasoning and hesitating—constant urging and solicitation of the mind to act, and as constant an escape from action; ceaseless reproaches of himself for sloth and negligence, while the whole energy of his resolution evaporates in these reproaches. This, too, not from cowardice, for he is drawn as one of the bravest of his time—not from want of forethought or slowness of apprehension, for he sees through the very souls of all who surround him, but merely from that aversion to action which prevails among such as have a world in themselves."

—from Edgar Allan Poe's *Marginalia, ca.* 1845.

"In all commentating upon Shakespeare there has been a radical error never yet mentioned. It is the error of attempting to expound his characters—to account for their actions—to reconcile his inconsistencies—not as if they were the coinage of a human brain, but as if they had been actual existencies upon earth. We talk of Hamlet the man, instead of Hamlet the *dramatis persona*—of Hamlet that God, in place of Hamlet that Shakespeare, created. If Hamlet had really lived, and if the tragedy were an accurate record of his deeds, from this record (with some trouble) we might, it is true, reconcile his inconsistencies, and settle to our satisfaction his true character. But the task becomes the purest absurdity when we deal only with a phantom. It is not (then) the inconsistencies of the acting man which we have as a subject of discussion—(although we proceed as if it were, and thus *inevitably* err), but the whims and vacillations—the conflicting energies and indolences of the poet. It seems to us little less than a miracle that this obvious point should have been overlooked."

—from A. C. Bradley's *Shakespearean Tragedy,* 1904.

". . . Hamlet had speculative genius without being a philosopher, just as he had imaginative genius without being a poet. Doubtless in happier days he was a close and constant observer of men and manners . . . Again and again we remark that passion for generalization, which so occupied him, for instance, in reflections suggested by the King's drunkenness that he quite forgot what it was he was waiting to meet upon the battlements. Doubtless, too, he was always considering things, as Horatio thought, too curiously [*carefully*]. There was a necessity in his soul driving him to penetrate below the surface and to question what others took for granted. That fixed habitual look which the world wears for most men did not exist for him. He was forever unmaking his world and rebuilding it in thought, dissolving what to others were solid facts, and discovering what to others were old truths. There were no old truths for Hamlet. . . .

". . . Under conditions of a peculiar kind, Hamlet's reflectiveness certainly might prove dangerous to him, and his genius might even (to exaggerate a little) become his doom. Suppose that violent shock to his moral being of which I spoke; and suppose that under this shock, any possible action being denied to him, he began to sink into melancholy; then, no doubt, his imaginative and generalising habit of mind might extend the effects of this shock through his whole being and mental world. And if, the state of melancholy being thus deepened and fixed, a sudden demand for difficult and decisive action in a matter connected with the melancholy arose, this state might well have for one of its symptoms an endless and futile mental dissection of the required deed. And, finally, the futility of this process, and the shame of his delay, would further weaken him and enslave him to his melancholy still more. Thus the speculative habit would be *one* indirect cause of the morbid state which hindered action; and it would also reappear in a degenerate form as one of the *symptoms* of this morbid state. . . .

"And this is the time which his fate chooses. In this hour of uttermost weakness, this sinking of his whole being towards annihilation, there comes on him, bursting the bounds of the natural world with a shock of astonishment and terror, the revelation of his mother's adultery and his father's murder, and, with this, the demand on him, in the name of everything dearest and most sacred, to arise and act. And for a moment, though his brain reels and totters, his soul leaps up in passion to answer this demand. But it comes too late. It does [but] strike home the last rivet in the melancholy which holds him bound . . . and the rest of the story exhibits his vain efforts to fulfil this duty, his unconscious self-excuses and unavailing self-reproaches, and the tragic results of his delay. . . .

"I have dwelt thus at length on Hamlet's melancholy because, from the psychological point of view, it is the centre of the tragedy, and to omit it from consideration or to underrate its intensity is to make Shakespeare's story unintelligible. But the psychological point of view is not equivalent to the tragic; and having once given its due weight to the fact of Hamlet's melancholy, we may freely admit, or rather may be anxious to insist, that this pathological condition would excite but little, if any, interest if it were not the condition of a nature distinguished by that speculative genius on which the Schlegel-Coleridge type of theory lays stress. Such theories misinterpret the connection between that genius and Hamlet's failure, but still it is this connection which gives to his story its peculiar fascination and makes it appear (if the phrase may be allowed) as the symbol of a tragic mystery inherent in human nature. . . .

"In this mood, on his way to his mother's chamber, he comes upon the King, alone, kneeling, conscience-stricken and attempting to pray. . . . That this again is an unconscious excuse for delay is now pretty generally agreed, and it is needless to describe again the state of mind which, on the view explained in our last lecture, is the real cause of Hamlet's failure here. The first five words he utters, 'Now might I do it,' show that he has no effective *desire* to 'do it'; and in the little sentences that follow, and the long pauses between them, the endeavour at a resolution, and the sickening return of melancholic paralysis, however difficult a task they set to the actor, are plain enough to a reader. . . . But in one point the great majority of critics, I think, go astray. The feeling of intense hatred which Hamlet expresses is not the cause of his sparing the King, and in his heart he knows this; but it does not at all follow that this feeling is unreal. All the evidence afforded by the play goes to show that it is perfectly genuine, and I see no reason whatever to doubt that Hamlet would have been very sorry to send his father's murderer to heaven, nor much to doubt that he would have been glad to send him to perdition."

Appendix

A. The Melancholy Humor.

The problems of understanding Hamlet's character and interpreting his tragedy are complicated perhaps chiefly by two elements of the play, Hamlet's actual case of melancholia when the play begins and his pretended madness (*antic disposition*) after he has met the Ghost. (The relation between these two is also discussed in the "Commentary" on I.5). The two elements are closely related in several ways, but are nevertheless distinguishable.

Let us begin with the melancholy.[1] In the physiological and psychological theory of the humors prevalent down to the eighteenth century, melancholy is the medical name of the black bile, a thick, black, sluggish moistness or humor, "the dregs of the blood." Like the other humors, it possesses some universal physical qualities: Melancholy is cold and dry. (*Dry* here is the equivalent to *thick*.) It is produced in the liver from the substance called *chyle*, the result of primary digestion in the stomach. Melancholy, though semiexcremental, gives nourishment to the spleen and the bones. Therefore, it is a normal part of man's physique.

The black bile, or melancholy, has no distinct effect on behavior when all four humors exist and function in right proportion in the body. (The other three are, of course, blood, bile, and phlegm.) However, if by the dominance of some habit such as inactivity or of wrong diet or especially of the passions of fear or sorrow, the melancholy humor is increased in the body, then psychological results become evident. The humor not only *results from,* but in turn *causes,* the passions of fear and sorrow. These passions are the characteristic mark of the melancholy temperament, or disposition in which the humor has the ascendancy. Of course the melancholy person also shows other familiar symptoms such as insomnia, unsociability, lethargy, and suspicion. Less familiar ones are jealousy, peevishness, restlessness. In advanced cases, the victim has hallucinations.

In physical appearance the melancholy man is pallid or sallow of complexion and emaciated, and because of his introversion, he is neglectful of his grooming and clothing.

Another aspect of the disease is to be mentioned—*melancholy adust* (*ad-ustum,* "burnt up"). Any prolonged violent passion, because of the heat which it engenders in the body, may consume any of the humors (except phlegm) leaving a dark residue called melancholy adust. Even a small quantity of this substance in the body produces an advanced case of melancholia with suicidal impulses. Melancholy adust is indistinguishable from the normal melancholy humor except that it is more virulent.

Unquestionably Hamlet is melancholy at the beginning of the play and profoundly so after the visit with the Ghost. The only classical symptom not suggested or shown is fear, a passion that would deprive him of all heroism. His sorrow, or grief, is obvious. Professor Babb instances also his unsociability, his "morose brooding, his weary despondency, his suicidal impulses, his cynical satire, his sudden changes of mood," and his painful circumspection about the revenge. His "apathetic and cynical disillusionment" is paralleled in other melancholiacs of the drama.[2]

All of this, though part of it is unfamiliar theory, would offer no extreme difficulty for the modern reader or audience, were it not complicated by Hamlet's assuming an antic disposition. Professor Babb says that traditionally the revenger in Elizabethan tragedy was likely "to utilize his abnormality [of mind], even to exaggerate it" to deceive others as to his helplessness and harmlessness. Now, "in Renaissance science the distinction between melancholy and madness is rather one of degree than of kind."[3] Hence we may sum up the situation by saying that Hamlet's antic disposition is the display of certain mental symptoms of melancholia very highly exaggerated. The rudeness he shows to all except Horatio after Act I, the caustic satires against women and old men, these may be considered extreme developments of the unsociability, suspicion, and peevishness characteristic of melancholy. The "malcontent type" is a dramatic development from basic qualities of melancholy; and malcontent railing becomes, when it has lost rationality in madness, the crude satire that Hamlet uses.

In effect, then, Hamlet's state is genuine melancholy disguised, much of the time, by melancholy-mad behavior. Yet fundamentally the hero is sane. Shakespeare's distinction between verse and prose may help us to see the truth here. Shakespeare seems to use prose or very irregular verse for mad utterances. Blank verse is kept for sane people. Study this distinction in *Hamlet* and note that the scenes of antic disposition are in prose.

Appendix

This short analysis may have discovered two roots of our difficulty in interpreting the sane character of Hamlet. One is that we have lost our familiarity with the traditional signs of melancholy madness in Elizabethan drama and hence confuse Hamlet's pretense with reality. The other is that any character veiled by two layers of abnormality, one real (melancholy) and one pretended (madness) is bound to be very obscure at times.

B. *The Quartos and First Folio.*

We can only know what Shakespeare intended us to see in *Hamlet* from what Shakespeare wrote into it; and though this statement sounds all too obvious, yet it has to be kept in mind when we consider the texts of *Hamlet*. Three versions of the tragedy seem to have some *authority,* that is, a near connection with Shakespeare's manuscript or manuscripts. Since these three editions differ markedly from one another, the problem of scholars today is to explain these differences and reconstruct the text of *Hamlet* as they think Shakespeare would approve it. This difficulty is not diminished by the thought that the *Hamlet* Shakespeare approved as produced at the Globe surely differed from the *Hamlet* Shakespeare had written at home. Let us not consider any further the theoretical goals of editing, but turn to the practical problems confronting editor, producer, and critic when they grapple with the text of *Hamlet*.

Four quarto editions of the tragedy were printed before 1623, but as the third and fourth are reprints of the second, they have little importance for us. In the parlance of Shakespeare study, a quarto is a single edition of one of the plays in a format which at that time measured about seven by ten inches.[4] The First Quarto of *Hamlet,* published in 1603, gives a version of the play differing in striking ways from the later, more authentic texts. It omits so much that it is only a little more than half as long as they; the names of some of the characters are different; and the language is often notably inferior. For such reasons it is called the Bad Quarto. It is only rarely helpful in determining the ideal text of *Hamlet.* Very probably the Bad Quarto was printed from a manuscript made by an actor (or actors) who had played in the tragedy in an earlier version than Shakespeare's revision of around 1600. It is, therefore, a "memorial reconstruction," the product of the actor's imperfect knowledge of parts which he himself had not taken, as well as his own parts.

In the following year, 1604, was published the Second, or Good,

Quarto, as if to replace the Bad one in the public's attention. We cannot infer from this close sequence that Shakespeare got permission from his fellow actors to publish this authentic version; we have no evidence on that. But we surely can infer that the Lord Chamberlain's Men consented to the new edition; very possibly they initiated it. The Second Quarto contains about 218 lines absent from the Folio *Hamlet,* and, though it also lacks about 85 lines found in the Folio, it is not only longer, but probably closer to Shakespeare's manuscript of the play as first read to the Chamberlain's Men. There is strong evidence that the printer of the Second Quarto had in his hands either Shakespeare's own autograph manuscript or a scribe's transcript that closely followed Shakespeare's spelling and punctuation. It is therefore an edition of very high authority. The statistics about the number of lines in the Second Quarto and Folio give one no more than a hint of the vast number of other differences in phrases and single words, not to speak of spelling and punctuation. In fact, the comparison of these two versions (their collation) is the huge task of the editor of *Hamlet.*

A folio is a very large book, usually too heavy to hold in the hands for reading; a support is needed. The First Folio of Shakespeare (1623) is a thick volume of double-column pages offering the world all the plays of which Shakespeare's fellow actors believed Shakespeare was largely the author. The version of *Hamlet* in the Folio has seemed to most scholars to have been printed from a manuscript that either had served as promptbook at the Globe, or had been copied from the promptbook. Inasmuch as Shakespeare was acting and helping to produce at the time when *Hamlet* came to the Globe, we have strong (though not conclusive) grounds for assuming that cuts and other changes in the Folio *Hamlet,* as compared to the Second Quarto version, were made with the author's permission, if not on his initiative. (Yet we ought to remember that *Hamlet* may have been produced a number of times even after Shakespeare had retired from the theater, though we have no record of production. A reprint quarto was published in 1611.)

The nature of the verbal differences, or variants, between the Folio and Second Quarto suggests to most editors that the Folio manuscript was certainly not in Shakespeare's handwriting and very likely was descended through one or two scribal copies from it. Consequently, editors often prefer the variants in the Second Quarto. For instance, at IV.4.8 Shakespeare probably wrote *Go*

Appendix

softly *on*, not *Go* safely *on;* for Fortinbras is not fearful of danger, but intends to march slowly for a time, while waiting for the Captain to return with the King's permission to advance. A glance at the textual notes on any page of your copy of *Hamlet* will probably demonstrate this editorial preference for Quarto variants.

But the usual practice in modern editions is to conflate the Second Quarto and Folio versions; the Folio is adopted as basic, and then the Quarto is drawn upon, usually quite fully, for improvements and additions. In lecture your instructor will probably discuss in some detail the passages where an editor has to make a doubtful choice between Quarto and Folio.

C. For Further Reading.

The immense bibliography of *Hamlet* studies and criticism (see "To the Student," above) makes any suggestion for further reading appear absurdly inadequate. However, you may find the following works of criticism enlightening to you. They are arranged by date of publication, latest first.

L. C. Knights, *An Approach to "Hamlet,"* 1960. Hamlet retreats from life.

Harry Levin, *The Question of Hamlet,* 1959.

William Empson, *"Hamlet* When New," *The Sewanee Review,* XLI (1953), 15-42, 185-205. A stimulating article.

Maynard Mack, "The World of *Hamlet," The Yale Review,* XLI (1952), 502-523. Often deservedly reprinted.

C. C. H. Williamson, *Readings on the Character of Hamlet,* 1950.

John Dover Wilson, *What Happens in Hamlet,* 1935.

T. S. Eliot, "Hamlet and His Problems," *Selected Essays 1917-1932,* 1932.

G. Wilson Knight, "The Embassy of Death," *The Wheel of Fire,* 1930.

A. C. Bradley, *Shakespearean Tragedy,* 1903.

Notes

The Persons of the Play

[1] To argue that Claudius is not really a usurper, because he has been duly elected, largely ignores the Elizabethan view that Claudius's murder of King Hamlet disqualified Claudius as a candidate for the Kingship. Macbeth also was duly elected; but Macduff calls him a usurper, V.8.55. Hamlet in his brief tenure of the throne at the end not only predicts that Fortinbras will succeed him, but approves the choice. This re-establishment of a legal succession must be significant.

[2] The contrast between Hamlet and Fortinbras involves, of course, only the mentally sick Hamlet, not the normal Prince, whom we never meet, even in Act V. The contrast is introduced partly for the pain it gives to Hamlet himself as he thinks about it.

"A Commentary on the Action"

[1] When Lewis Theobald localized the setting as *a platform* in 1733, the word meant 'a paved terrace.'

[2] Note the square brackets in most editions, showing the omission of 108-125 from the Folio version.

[3] Perhaps *cross it* means 'make the sign of the cross toward it,' in order to see the spirit's response—of gratitude, if it is a soul from Purgatory; anger, if a demon. But the other sense of *cross* is more likely.

[4] In the Second Quarto the stage direction, after listing the other entrants, ends with *Hamlet, cum Aliis,* 'Hamlet with others.'

[5] A Freudian interpretation of Hamlet's character (e.g., that he has an anti-Oedipus complex) does not affect the political aspects of his situation.

[6] In Elizabethan times no one could travel abroad without special permission from the Privy Council, because of the danger of defecting to Catholicism or to the service of Spain.

[7] Of course Claudius's usurpation (as it seems to Hamlet) is also an unkind, i.e., unnatural, cruelty.

[8] The sense 'murder' is a modern meaning based upon *Hamlet,* because we know what Hamlet does not know.

[9] Considering the tone of the preceding sentences in the advice, the baser meaning, or at least the ambiguity, is what Shakespeare probably intended. But note that G. L. Kittredge thinks that Polonius's advice is "sound and sensible—not more 'worldly-wise' than the occasion war-

Notes

rants." *Hamlet* (1939), 155. He cites *All's Well That Ends Well*, I.1.70-79, among many other parallels. However, the Countess's advice to her son urges a far higher virtue and ends with a promise of prayer. Compare the two passages.

[10] Marriage to Ophelia would certainly cure Hamlet's melancholy if love were the cause of his illness. But at this point Polonius does not concern himself with the melancholy at all. Later he decides love is the cause, II.2.145-151.

[11] About two months later Polonius says he did speak of it! See II.2.141-142. Obviously, Shakespeare does not expect the audience to remember whether it was Polonius or Laertes that mentioned the idea.

[12] Some critics suspect that Claudius plans to save Ophelia to be his own prey. Although such a plan may be in character, no other part of the play gives evidence of Claudius's lust for Ophelia. Hamlet's remark in II.2.185-187 probably does not refer specifically to the King. Claudius's fear of Hamlet is sufficient basis for his warning to Polonius.

[13] Probably the King's (formerly the Lord Chamberlain's) Men cut lines 17-38 mainly because of the assertion that Danes were notorious for drunkenness. After 1603 the Queen of England, James's consort, was Anne of Denmark. Although the idea that the Scandinavians, Dutch, and Germans were drunkards was widespread in England, Shakespeare's emphasis on it was untactful. It was not so under Queen Elizabeth.

[14] For instance, F. T. Bowers, "Hamlet as Scourge and Minister," *PMLA*, LXX (1955), 740-749, and L. C. Knights, *An Approach to Hamlet*, 1960.

[15] For (2) see Sister Miriam Joseph, *"Hamlet:* Christian Tragedy," *Studies in Philology*, LIX (1962), 119-140; for (3), Paul N. Siegel, "Discerning the Ghost in *Hamlet*," *PMLA*, LXXVIII (1963), 148-149.

[16] One of the more persuasive statements is that of R. H. West, "Kings Hamlet's Ambiguous Ghost," *PMLA*, LXX (1955), 1107-1117, who argues that Shakespeare deliberately left the nature of the Ghost uncertain because in real life this would be the Prince's impression. (But that the Ghost is an actual spirit and that its account is true are certain.)

[17] There is a semicolon after *mind* in the Folio.

[18] But acting tradition has him speak line 80.

[19] Lawrence Babb, *The Elizabethan Malady* (1951), 36. See also 108-109.

[20] The latter is Kittredge's suggestion, *Hamlet*, xiii. However, Peter Alexander explains that Hamlet uses the antic disposition to *reveal* to Claudius, by covert allusions, that he knows of the murder; for Hamlet is too noble to wish to take his enemy by surprise. *Hamlet Father and Son* (1955), 180.

[21] Ophelia might have said, "No hat upon his head or in his hand." Kittredge says, "Ophelia would have expected to see Hamlet at the door with his hat on, but he would remove it as he crossed the threshold." *Hamlet*, 177.

[22] No speeches in the play indicate that they have been at Wittenberg with Hamlet and Horatio.

[23] This idea underlies Robert Burton's massive *Anatomy of Melancholy*, 1621.

[24] Kittredge defends the diction of the opening as conventional and not odd. *Hamlet*, 182. (Keep in mind as you read Hamlet's verse that *doubt* means 'fear.')

[25] The scene is out of doors, 208.

[26] His rudeness to Polonius may be regarded as due partly to antic disposition, partly to resentment on very real grounds. For a short, pointed discussion of Hamlet's melancholy, see Babb, *Elizabethan Malady*, 106-110.

[27] "The Prince has no doubt lost his way," says C. S. Lewis, quoted in Knights, *Approach to Hamlet*, 44. "He does little effective thinking on the moral and metaphysical problems that beset him," adds Knights, 68.

[28] R. W. Battenhouse, "Hamlet's Apostrophe on Man: Clue to the Tragedy," *PMLA*, LXVI (1951), 1073-1113. At the end Hamlet is "a man without hope . . . Skepticism has overcome his bad dreams."

[29] In all this episode Denmark is forgotten; the English situation is in mind. And, curiously, the *tragedians of the city* (342) are "strolling" in the country—at Elsinore, the capital of Denmark!

[30] As both the north and the winds are associated with demons, Hamlet may be suggesting that at times he is possessed by a devil, a common view of madness.

[31] For Jephtha, see the Bible, *Judges*, XI:30-40.

[32] Babb, *Elizabethan Malady*, 107.

[33] Claudius's lines, 51-53, mean, "As the harlot's pocky skin is ugly compared to the paint she lays over it, so is my guilt hideous compared to my benevolent words."

[34] Some of the ideas in the soliloquy have been drawn, apparently, from Stoic writers, especially Plutarch and Cardan, a Renaissance moralist.

[35] It does not seem certain that Hamlet was unaware that the dumb-show was to be given; but as it does not upset his plans, whether he is surprised does not matter.

[36] Note *nephew* instead of *brother*, in 254. Probably this is a slip of the tongue due to excitement, but it might be significant to Claudius. Anyway, Claudius's question (242-243) seems to indicate his suspicion that Hamlet has chosen this play with knowledge of the King's guilt, and Hamlet's answer, *The Mouse-trap*, should confirm the suspicion.

[37] Maynard Mack, "The World of Hamlet," reprinted in L. Dean, *Shakespeare: Modern Essays in Criticism* (1957), 255.

[38] In the Folio the stage direction is simply *Enter King*.

[39] Note especially 25-29; in 26 *debate* means 'settle by fighting.'

Notes 89

The passage is certainly not clear, for the traditional belief that foreign war is healthful for nations seems contrary to the metaphor of *impostume,* 'abscess.' Probably we are to understand that Hamlet does not state his true feeling to the Captain, but withholds it until he is alone (53-56).

[40] It will not help Laertes's outraged sense of honor to learn that Hamlet has slain Polonius by a sudden attack on the old man, who has been caught in a defenceless position, and that the slayer has been sent overseas.

[41] Scholars are not agreed as to the location of the "grave trap" on the Elizabethan stage. Whether the one traditionally called by this name was in the inner stage (if that existed as an alcove) does not matter here; it seems clear that the Graveyard Scene in *Hamlet* must take place on the outer stage.

[42] An old stage tradition for the part.

[43] If we must have an explanation, we may suppose that Horatio has ridden far to meet Hamlet, they have ridden back together, and, still having many things to talk over, they have dismounted near Elsinore and walked through byways toward the castle.

[44] The severity of the Church on Ophelia is more a dramatic device than an imitation of real practice. Being irrational, Ophelia could not have been guilty of sinful self-destruction and in reality probably would not have been denied the usual rites. The details of the scene generally recall a Catholic ceremony; but the word *requiem* was used occasionally in the Anglican Church for a while after the Reformation.

[45] The stage direction in the Second Quarto mentions daggers with the foils. It was common for the contestants to fence with the rapier in the right hand, using a dagger in the left to parry some thrusts.

[46] Note that it is in blank verse, which is never used for Hamlet's antic disposition. Blank verse is also used in V.1.278-315, at the insulting of Laertes.

[47] In 262 *love* is used with the conventional politeness illustrated in formulas of introduction at that time, "I do beseech your love," etc. Hamlet's answer is polite, but curt. Laertes's response to the apology has been anticipated.

"A Summary of the Action"

[1] So Hamlet speaks of him, though we should expect *brother*. The speech headings label the other two characters *Player King* and *Player Queen*, not *Duke* and *Duchess*.

"Appendix"

[1] A full explanation of the psychology of humors will be found in Babb, *Elizabethan Malady,* Chapter I. To this book I am much indebted

for details in the present short note. A summary account of the humors will be found in my *Reading Shakespeare's Plays*, 49-53, and in many reference works.

[2] Pages 108-110.

[3] Pages 90-91.

[4] There is a short, general discussion of textual problems in *Reading Shakespeare's Plays*, 89-95.